Methods of Teaching
EDUCATIONAL PSYCHOLOGY

Methods of Teaching
EDUCATIONAL PSYCHOLOGY

Dr. T. Shankar

CRESCENT
PUBLISHING CORPORATION

[The responsibility for the facts stated, conclusions reached and plagiarism, if any, in this book is entirely that of the Author. And the Publisher bears no responsibility for them, whatsoever.]

Methods of Teaching Educational Psychology

***Reprint*: 2015**

ISBN 81-8342-061-3

Published by :

CRESCENT PUBLISHING CORPORATION
4831/24, Prahlad Street,
Ansari Road, Darya Ganj,
New Delhi - 110002
Ph. : 23272541, 23257835
Fax : 91- 011- 23257835
e-mail : campusbooks@hotmail.com

Printed at :
Roshan Offset Printers
Delhi

Preface

Educational psychology is the study of how humans learn in educational settings, the effectiveness of educational interventions, the psychology of teaching, and the social psychology of schools as organisations. It informs a wide range of specialities within educational studies, including instructional design, educational technology, curriculum development, organisational learning, special education and classroom management. Educational psychology both draws from and contributes to cognitive science and the learning sciences.

Over the years, educational psychologists study learning and teaching and, at the same time, strive to improve educational practice. Educational psychology has been a part of teacher preparation, moving from a centrepiece in many programs, through periods when it was deemed irrelevant by some, to current concerns about its role in the reforming of teacher education and teaching. Today, psychological knowledge is used to ground reforms in teaching a'nd schooling, particularly the call for teaching for understanding. Current standards for teacher certifications and suggestions for reform in teacher education assume that teachers will have a deep and generative understanding of learning, development, motivation, and individual differences.

The 21st century marks a critical time for education and educational psychology faculty. Courses in teacher education and educational psychology provide students with a breadth of concepts, theory, and research, but often in a decontextualised way. It is essential that teacher education programmes clearly articulate the mission and the objectives of teacher education and engage in rigorous inquiry demonstrating their effectiveness.

This thoughtful book provides a comprehensive account of the methods and strategies of teaching educational psychology. It is designed for a variety of audience including pre-service and in-service teachers, administrators, policy-makers, researchers, students, practitioners in educational psychology and the public.

Dr. T. Shankar

Contents

1

Teaching of Educational Psychology

Educational psychology is the study of how humans learn in educational settings, the effectiveness of educational interventions, the psychology of teaching, and the social psychology of schools as organisations. Although the terms "educational psychology" and "school psychology" are often used interchangeably, researchers and theorists are likely to be identified as educational psychologists, whereas practitioners in schools or school-related settings are identified as school psychologists. Educational psychology is concerned.with the processes of educational attainment among the general population and sub-populations such as gifted children and those subject to specific disabilities.

Educational psychology can in part be understood through its relationship with other disciplines. It is informed primarily by psychology, bearing a relationship to that discipline analogous to the relationship between medicine and biology. Educational psychology in turn informs a wide range of specialities within educational studies, including instructional design, educational technology, curriculum development, organisational learning, special education and classroom management. Educational psychology both draws from and contributes to cognitive science and the learning sciences. In universities, departments of educational psychology are usually housed within faculties of education, possibly accounting for the lack of representation of educational psychology content in introductory psychology textbooks.

To understand the characteristics of learners in childhood, adolescence, adulthood, and old age, educational psychology develops and applies theories of human development. Often cast as stages through which people pass as they mature, developmental theories describe changes in mental abilities, social roles, moral reasoning, and beliefs about the nature of knowledge. For example, educational psychologists have researched the instructional applicability of Jean Piaget's theory of development, according to which children mature through four stages of cognitive capability. Piaget hypothesised that children are not capable of abstract logical thought until they are older than about 11 years, and therefore younger children need to be taught using concrete objects and examples. Researchers have found that transitions, such as from concrete to abstract logical thought, do not occur at the same time in all domains. A child may be able to think abstractly about mathematics, but remain limited to concrete thought when reasoning about human relationships. Perhaps Piaget's most enduring contribution is his insight that people actively construct their understanding through a self-regulatory process.

Piaget proposed a developmental theory of moral reasoning in which children progress from a naive understanding of morality based on behavior and outcomes to a more advanced understanding based on intentions. Piaget's views of moral development were elaborated by Kohlberg into a stage theory of moral development. There is evidence that the moral reasoning described in stage theories is not sufficient to account for moral behavior. For example, other factors such as modeling are required to explain bullying.

Developmental theories are sometimes presented not as shifts between qualitatively different stages, but as gradual increments on separate dimensions. Development of epistemological beliefs have been described in terms gradual changes in people's belief in: certainty and permanence of knowledge, fixedness of ability, and credibility of authorities such as teachers and experts. People develop more sophisticated beliefs about knowledge as they gain in education and maturity.

IMPORTAMCE OF TEACHING EDUCATIONAL PSYCHOLOGY

The need to do, and share, research on the teaching of educational psychology is based in the structure and purpose of the discipline itself. Since the infamous conflicts between Dewey and Thorndike a century ago, educational psychologists have continually debated the nature of the relationship between and the appropriate proportion of emphasis on the science of psychology, on the one hand, and the practice of education on the other. At times, the pendulum has swung so far toward one direction or the other that the very existence of the discipline, as distinct from either parent field, has come into question.

Yet throughout a century of debate on the appropriate topics, methods, and uses of research in educational psychology, the overarching purpose of the discipline has remained remarkably constant: to improve education. As Wittrock asserted in 1992, "Educational Psychology is distinct from other branches of psychology because it has the understanding and improvement of education as its primary goal." In her latest edition of *Educational Psychology,* perhaps the best-selling textbook in the field today, Anita Woolfolk states unequivocally that, "Both in the past and today, educational psychologists study learning and teaching and, at the same time, strive to improve educational practice". Thus, unlike many sciences, and even many branches of psychology, the fulfillment of the very purpose and goal of educational psychology depends upon the effective communication and use of its findings to and by a wide variety of people outside the discipline itself, all those who regulate, administer, and actually practice education-it depends, in fact, on the teaching of educational psychology.

The word teach applies to any manner of imparting information or skill so that others may learn. Certainly, educational psychology is often taught, and taught effectively, in the traditional undergraduate college classroom. Indeed, a class in educational psychology has long been considered one of the "foundations" of preservice teacher education, and much of our own work in this area has been done in this context. However, especially in the rapidly changing landscape of education today, inservice teachers, too, need structured opportunities to learn and think about such matters as student motivation, assessment, and the impact of various forms of student diversity on learning, all traditional topics in educational psychology.

Due to a desire for more "practical" learning, plus the inconveniences of timing and transportation, many in-service teachers choose to learn not in college classrooms, but through non-traditional forms of instruction, including intense summer or weekend workshops, distance learning, proprietary software programs, or onsite, collegial professional development groups. Yet we know relatively little about how to teach educational psychology in these new contexts, nor about how to help teachers learn principles of learning and instruction as they teach in their own classrooms, potentially ideal sites for situated learning through teacher action research and design experiments.

And teachers are not our only potential "students." For at least a decade there have been calls for educational psychologists to "teach" our most reliable findings and bestsupported theories to policymakers and politicians at all levels, in the modest hope that our work can help "illuminate some of the educational issues" facing society today. Indeed, In the No Child Left Behind Act, the government of the United States has committed itself to developing educational policy based on "educational practices supported by rigorous evidence" of just the sort offered by educational psychology. We urgently need to learn more about how to communicate the basics of our discipline, its methods, theories and findings, clearly and effectively to these "others" – administrators, school boards, and legislators-so that they "may learn" the knowledge they need to make good decisions about educational policy. And in this case, as in many other educational contexts, motivating the students to learn may be an essential first step in good teaching.

Jeanne Ormrod maintains that we need to extend our teaching even further, that "to have the greatest impact on educational decision making, we must enter the picture not at the problem-solving stage, and not even at the problem-identification stage, but at the very beginning, at the acquisition-of-beliefs stage". She suggests that we "bring basic concepts and tenets of educational psychology into mainstream national culture" by going to PTA and School Board meetings, writing Letters to the Editor in the local newspaper, and learning to value articles in "magazines and journals with a large readership" such as Reader's Digest, Parents Magazine and Psychology Today as much as we value articles that are "highly abstract and steeped in jargonese" in professional "journals and other venues that only we ourselves read". Yet again, we know little or nothing about how to so "teach" our subject to the public, to the taxpayers, voters and parents to whom the policymakers are ultimately responsive and responsible.

A final group of potential students for our discipline are the students in our schools. Given long-established findings regarding the importance of metacognition and self-regulation to learning, it seems likely that older students, at least, could greatly benefit from a class in practical educational psychology, including structured opportunities to reflect on their own developmental paths, ways of learning, and patterns of motivation. Such a class might best be offered outside of the school setting, in an after-school or community-based program, to avoid potential self-consciousness in the students and perhaps even conflicts of interest on the part of the teachers.

Case Method in Teaching Educational Psychology

The 21st century marks a critical time for education and educational psychology faculty. It is essential that teacher education programs clearly articulate the mission and the objectives of teacher education and engage in rigorous inquiry demonstrating their effectiveness. Teacher education programs, like other professional degree programs, face the challenge of demonstrating the relevance of empirical theories provided in the college classroom to everyday practice in the "real world."

Courses in teacher education and educational psychology provide students with a breadth of concepts, theory, and research, but often in a decontextualised way.

Particularly in introductory courses, there is a wealth of information on an array of topics, all of which can potentially assist teachers in their practices. However, the pressure to cover material coupled with a traditional lecture or whole class discussion approach can prevent future teachers from actively connecting the theories and concepts taught to practice. The case method represents an instructional approach that can assist faculty in education to better meet some of their goals in this area.

The case method, which attempts to bridge the chasm between theory and practice, is an instructional technique widely used in business, nursing, and law. Professional schools find that cases provide contexts in which theories and concepts can be tested, discussed, applied or challenged. Cases are defined differently across and within disciplines. Generally speaking, a case is any situation or set of situations in which a person or persons are engaged in an activity that reflects real-life practice in a particular domain.

In education settings, cases can come in the form of dilemmas written from the perspective of a teacher, videotaped instructional sessions, or hypothetical scenarios where multiple stakeholders wrestle with a teaching and learning dilemma. The case itself is not an instructional technique, but rather the case sets the stage for peer discussion and case analysis. The case method approach should reflect an engaged learning environment where students present their perspectives, hear the perspectives of their peers, and apply the theories covered in class.

The case method is not, however, simply a tool to prove that academia is relevant to practitioners. This method also fosters student reflection on preconceived notions and promotes changes in thinking via a constructivist approach to learning. Engaging in debate and dialogue with their peers about a situational problem promotes critical thinking in students. An effective case discussion leader elicits multiple perspectives and solutions, while making reference to the theoretical and conceptual underpinnings of the case. The discussion occurs mainly among the students, with the facilitator guiding, summarising, and reflecting on the objectives of instruction throughout. Much of the research on the case method in education focuses narrowly on "how best to" teach using cases or studying the impact of case-based instruction on college students' thinking, reasoning, and in a few cases their practice.

Data for these studies come mainly from examining student case analyses or student generated cases. While these are important areas of inquiry, it is possible that the results reflect improvement in student mastery of instructor requirements and not necessarily true growth in cognition, reflection, and reasoning. Students are likely to improve in the quality of their written case analyses over the course of the semester based on instructor feedback, clarity of instructor expectations for assignments, and experiences working with cases. If it is purported that the case method directly or indirectly impacts teacher preparation and effectiveness in the classroom,. as has been asserted in other professional fields,, then research needs to assess the extent to which exposure and engagement in the case method extends beyond the students' abilities to adequately complete a case analysis of a teaching dilemma.

Researchers have examined a number of essential elements for effective case method instruction. In addition to studying the procedural aspects of the case method, there is a growing body of research that examines the impact of the case method on student outcomes. In a comprehensive review of research on the case method in teacher education,

Smith found three categories of outcomes measured, including changes in students' cognition, reflection, and pedagogical knowledge.

The case-method has been touted as an instructional approach that challenges teacher education students' thinking and their abilities to transfer what they are learning to the classroom setting. Several studies have examined students' cognitive growth throughout a semester-long course that used the case method as the primary pedagogical approach. These studies on cognitive change shared some common approaches. Each study employed multiple qualitative methods to qualify or quantify changes, as evidenced in students' written analysis of cases, from the beginning to the end of a semester.

Many courses and programs state that students will improve their skills in reflection as a result of taking a course or graduating from a teacher education program. Researchers hove found that case method instruction can help students' become more reflective thinkers by encouraging them to consider critically the decisions of actors in a case and use evidence to support their assumptions about the case.

For example, Hewitt, Pedretti, Bencze, Dale Vaillancourt, and Yoon examined elementary education students' conceptions of reflection while engaged in a videocase lesson. Harrington, Quinn-Leering, and Hodson studied 21 elementary education students' written case analyses for evidence of critical reflection. Reichelt's studied how the case-method affected 14 secondary foreign language students' reflection, decision-making, and problem-solving abilities. These studies all revealed moderate changes in the reflective practices of the students at the end of the respective courses.

Use of Picture Books in Teaching Educational Psychology

Courses in educational psychology are the theoretical backbone of college preparation programs for students seeking degrees and/or certification for jobs that that lead to careers with children. While students are usually enthusiastic about taking practicum courses because they provide hands-on activities for immediate and direct use, they are often less enthusiastic about studying theories about cognition, moral and social development, and motivation. Enthusiasm may wane because students do not see the practicality of theory or understand how it applies to their immediate needs.

Typically, educational psychology courses are taught in a lecture format, and this also can make theories seem dry and removed from real life. To appreciate the practical nature of educational psychology theory, students must bridge the gap between what they learn in their courses and their interactions with children in the field. One way to do this, as the opening scenario shows, is to enrich lectures and course work with well-chosen picture books.

Researchers and instructors have discovered the motivating appeal and cognitive benefits of children's literature for students of all ages and abilities. We are partial to children's picture books because they are entertaining, can be read and discussed in a short period of time, and when carefully selected, present theory accurately in both words and pictures. Sipe calls this textpicture relationship "synergy" because it is neither the text nor the illustration that creates understanding but a combination of the two. Images contribute to a deeper understanding of text, and text helps one see and learn from the images. Along these same lines, Mitchell uses the term "imagery-text" to convey the cognitive advantages of an image juxtaposed with the text. Text and image converge to become multi-modal input, and this is a powerful way to learn. When learning is energised, motivation is enhanced.

Motivational and Cognitive Benefits

Many people think of picture books as simple texts for beginning readers. Parents read picture books to children at bedtime and primary teachers use picture books in early childhood education. This may have been true in the past, but contemporary picture books have emerged as a key literary form within children's literature, and as a source of enjoyment and inspiration for people of all ages.

Smallwood is another instructor who advocates the use of picture books in the college classroom. Smallwood uses the "synergy" of picture books to teach literacy skills to her adult English language learners. She uses the stories to provide insight into the customs and concepts of a new culture, and she uses illustrations to visually depict new vocabulary terms and ideas. An example is her use of the dramatic illustrations in Brother Eagle, Sister Sky to, in her words, "convey the deeper meaning of the story, that is, respect for our environment".

College textbook writers recognise that picture books are powerful ways to illustrate concepts and ideas. The teacher's edition of Child Development suggests using Miss Rumphius to spark discussion about adolescent thinking and idealistic views. Fish is Fish is recommended in a book called How People Learn to help readers understand Piaget's concept of assimilation. The audience for picture books has broadened, and the use of picture books has expanded well beyond childhood.

Bruner notes that when learners see something happen, as well as read or hear about it, they encode this information both visually and verbally in their long-term memory. We agree with Bruner and find evidence for the cognitive benefits of picture books in the work of Paivio. According to Paivio's dual coding theory, two cognitive systems are used to process and store information: a verbal system for linguistic information and an imagery system for non-verbal input. Both language and images are stored independently and work together through associative cross-code links. Palvio's theory has since been confirmed with by neuroscience research, and it means that a word in the verbal system can spark an image and an image in the non-verbal system can prompt recall of a verbal fact.

Experiencing a picture book readaloud encourages dual encoding because the narrative provides verbal input while the illustrations show the concept in non-verbal form. Picture books are unique learning tools because they not only provide input in tandem but also do it contiguously in time. Mayer and Anderson call this the contiguity principle, and it supports our claim that picture books help students learn and understand theory at a deeper level. Contiguity of input helps students form a coherent mental model of theory in both images and words.

Historically, humans have enjoyed listening to and have learned about themselves and their world through story. Stories have been created in all human cultures, to explain natural forces, social contexts, and cultural mores. Thinking about story, in this broader sense of the word, emphasises how learning from narratives is an innately human, natural way of thinking, learning, and understanding what is important in one's world. Hearing the stories of others can provide individuals with vicarious experience and lead to insight beyond what is personally known. This is especially important when students lack background knowledge or practical experience to understand a theory and how it connects to the children with whom they are working. The stories we use with our students help them understand what a theory or concept looks, sounds, and feels like in the context of a character's experiences.

Effective teachers often use story intuitively when they teach. They use anecdotes, analogies, and metaphors to simplify and clarify concepts, make them more concrete, and build vocabulary. Instructors share personal experiences to enrich ideas presented in the classroom and students relate to that insider perspective. Deeper understanding occurs when a more knowledgeable other assists with vocabulary understanding and points out connections that bridge initial knowledge to life experiences. Picture books and focused discussions can be used to supplement presentation of theory and concepts, allow teachers to make their point without lecturing, challenge current ideas, and advance the reasoning skills of their students.

Proficient readers often ignore the illustrations in a picture book, focusing on the words rather than noticing how the message of the text is reinforced through the pictures. In doing so, they neglect three cognitive benefits: development of visual literacy, awareness of abstract concepts, and the use of imagery. Visual literacy, or the learning from pictures as well as from print, is dependent on analysis of illustrations within the context of the story. Promoting visual literacy teaches students to look at pictures for the details and information they contain. Students who develop this ability move beyond concrete, literal interpretations of what they see to deeper and more complex understandings of characters, contexts, and thoughts.

Encouraging the use of visual literacy helps students look beyond the surface to the deep complexity and subtleties that exist in the world. Abstract concepts can come to life through illustrations in tandem with text. Drawings allow students to see theory in the context of a character's experiences and interpret the reactions, responses, and decisions that a character may make.

The use of imagery allows learners to form mental representations in their mind and helps make theory more concrete. Neisser notes that imagery is constructive in nature and promotes active learning, deep processing, and superior recall. A picture is worth a thousand words, and supplementing course readings and lecture with the richness of illustration can be of cognitive benefit. Theory learned with story and illustrations is better understood, remembered, and transferred. This method is a powerful tool to enhance learning about theory, but finding and using picture books with adult learners takes know how, time, and skill.

Selection and Use

Key points to using picture books successfully with adult learners are a thorough knowledge of theory, access to picture books, and an ability to make connections between theory and appropriate books. Stories and illustrations should match the theory presented in a clear and well-defined way. Books should contain literary elements that encourage lively discussion, problem solving, and critical thinking. We like stories with human characters, or animal characters with decidedly human characteristics that display a wide range of cognitive, social, and emotional features.

When using picture books in our classrooms, we take steps to ensure that students can both hear the story and see the illustrations at the same time. Technology has helped us achieve this goal. If technology is not available, we achieve the same goal by obtaining multiple copies of the book, so small groups of students can examine the illustrations as we read aloud to the whole group.

Carefully selected books are used in five ways: to introduce theory, to build background knowledge, to make theory understandable, to create images of concepts and vocabulary terms, and to help students make connections between theory and their work with children.

To introduce theory: The opening scenario is an example of how we would use a picture book to introduce a theory. Students read an assigned section from the course textbook before presentation of the theory in class. To start the session, the book is read aloud and the illustrations are projected. During the readaloud, students discuss the story and pictures as we facilitate connections between theory, the story, and the children in their classrooms. This introductory session usually entails a book that provides a broad overview of the theory because our purpose is to engage students' thinking, discussion, and wondering about the finer points and nuances of the theory.

To build background knowledge: Sometimes introductory sessions reveal that students have read the course text but lack background knowledge or practical experience to understand what various theories are truly about and how they connect to the children they see. For example, students who teach young children may not understand ethological attachment theory, or how important toys and blankets can be to their young students when they are used as a secure base. Owen by Kevin Henkes presents this theory in appealing story form with delightful illustrations. A toddler named Owen attaches himself to a fuzzy yellow blanket to help self-regulate and manage stress as he experiences life's little stressors like "nail clippings and haircuts". Unfortunately, for Owen, his attachment to Fuzzy becomes a source of concern for his parents, and they try to wean him from his beloved blanket. The more they try, the more tensions arise and the more Owen needs Fuzzy. Eventually, a solution that respects both Owen's needs and those of his parents is discovered. The blanket is cut up into smaller pieces, like handkerchiefs, that Owen keeps to use as a secure base when he enters school. Attachment – the strong emotional bond between young children and their caregivers – is a key concept in understanding socio-emotional development, but students may not have experience with this concept in the context of a classroom.

To make theory more understandable: Besides using picture books to help students build background knowledge, we also use them make theory understandable by placing it in the context of a story and providing visual images of what to expect when working with children. For example, when we study memory, we provide small groups of students with a copy of Wilfred Gordon McDonald Partridge by Mem Fox. As a prereading activity we ask students to discuss what memory means to them. Then we have them read the book and look closely at the illustrations. This story is about a young boy named Wilfred Gordon who sets out to help ninety-six year old Miss Nancy find her fading memory. Because memory was a new concept, and an abstract one for a little boy, Wilfred Gordon solves the problem by talking to other people, like Mrs. Jordan, who tells him a memory is something warm. To make sense of this information, Wilfred Gordon takes a fresh, warm egg from under a hen and brings it to Miss Nancy. As she holds the warm egg, a smile crosses her face, and she begins to recall her lost memories. After finishing the story, we ask students to construct a definition of memory in the context of information processing and ways to enhance it with retrieval cues. We then explore memory strategies found in the course textbook, such as mnemonics, keywords, and acronyms.

To create images of concepts and vocabulary terms: The fourth way we use picture books is to help students form images of concepts and vocabulary terms associated with psychological theories. To help students understand the terms modeling and imitation as they are used in Bandura's social learning theory, we read Robert Munsch's Stephanie's Ponytail and vary our presentation style by not showing the pictures. We ask students to imagine how Stephanie styled her hair and how the other children imitated her. Then our students look at copies of the book in small groups and talk about what they had imagined and what the illustrations really look like. We then go on to introduce the pros and cons of imitation, the role models children follow today, and factors that influence observational learning, like a model's age, prestige, competence, or enthusiasm. Our students inevitably begin looking at the book's illustrations with a new eye, looking for evidence of accurate interpretation of theories of educational psychology in the pages of this children's picture book.

Piaget's notion of assimilation is often a difficult concept to explain and a difficult one for students to grasp and recall. Fish is Fish by Leo Lionni has become instrumental in helping our students understand this abstract concept. The story creates a visual referent for assimilation because it illustrates a fish's mental images as he assimilates new information heard about the world into his existing fishy scheme. When Fish hears about cows, he envisions them as large fish with horns and udders. When Fish hears about birds, he imagines them as flying fish with wings. Each of the Fish's mental representations is a slightly altered fish-like form that builds on his existing view of his world. The illustrations in this book provide a memorable visual of how the mind assimilates new information into an existing scheme.

To help students make connections between theory and their work with children: Learning theory removed from real life or not used to improve teaching is pointless; so is reading picture books aloud merely for the sake of a good story. Picture books are only effective as instructional aids when they help students make connections between what they learn in their educational psychology courses and the children in their lives.

2

Curriculum and Learning Assessment of Educational Psychology

Tradionally, because of their technical requirements, educational tests of any importance were seen as the province of statisticians and not that of teachers or subject matter specialists. Researchers conceptualizing effective teaching did not assign a significant role to assessment as part of the learning process. In traditional educational measurement courses, preservice teachers learned about domain specifications, item formats, and methods for estimating reliability and validity. Today assessment reformers emphasise the need for a closer substantive connection between assessment and meaningful instruction.

In describing present day practice, for example, Graue suggests that "assessment and instruction are conceived as curiously separate," a separation which Graue attributes to technical measurement concerns. A longer-term span of history, however, helps us to see that those measurement perspectives, now felt to be incompatible with instruction, came from an earlier, highly consistent theoretical framework in which conceptions of "scientific measurement" were closely aligned with curricula underpinned by behaviorist learning theory and directed at social efficiency. Figure 1 was devised to show in broad brush the shift from the dominant twentieth-century paradigm (on the left) to an emergent, constructivist paradigm (on the right), in which teachers' close assessment of students' understandings, feedback from peers, and student self-assessment are a part of the social processes that mediate the development of intellectual abilities, construction of knowledge, and formation of students' identities. The middle portion of the figure, intended to represent present-day teaching practices, adapts a similar figure from Graue showing a sphere for instruction entirely separate from the sphere for assessment.

According to this model, instruction and assessment are guided by different philosophies and are separated in time and place. Even classroom assessments, nominally under the control of teachers, may be more closely aligned with external tests than with day-to-day instructional activities. Although there is ample evidence that the intermediate model describes current practice, this model has no theoretical adherents. The best way to understand this mismatch is to see that instructional practices are guided by the new paradigm, while traditional testing practices are held over from the old.

Traditional Perspectuves of Curriculum, Psychology, and Measurement

It is important to know where traditional views of testing came from and to appreciate how tightly entwined they are with past models of curriculum and instruction, because new theories are defined and understood in contrast to prior theories. More importantly, however, dominant theories of the past continue to operate as the default framework

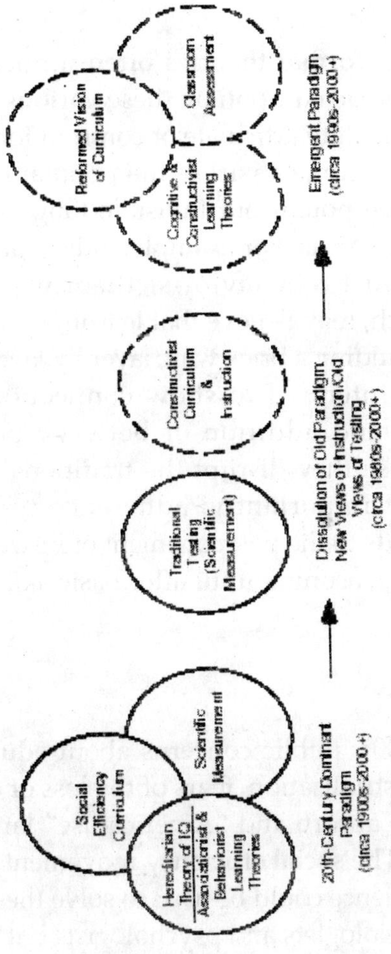

Figure 1. An historical overview illustrating how changing conceptions of curriculum, learning theory, and measurement explain the current incompatibility between new views of instruction and traditional views of testing.

affecting current practices and perspectives. Belief systems of teachers, parents, and policy makers are not exact reproductions of formal theories. They are developed through personal experience and from popular cultural beliefs.

Nonetheless, formal theories often influence implicit theories held and acted upon by these various groups; and because it is difficult to articulate or confront formal theories once they have become a part of the popular culture, their influence may be potent but invisible long after they are abandoned by theorists. For example, individuals who have been influenced by behaviorist theories, even if not identified as such, may believe that learning in an academic subject is like building a brick wall, layer by layer. They may resist reforms intended to show connections between multiplication and addition or between patterns and functions because they disrupt the traditional sequencing of topics. Most importantly, adherence to behaviorist assumptions leads to the postponement of instruction aimed at thinking and reasoning until after basic skills have been mastered.

Social Efficiency

In the early 1900s, public concerns about education were shaped by industrialisation, fears of the loss of community, and the need to absorb and "Americanise" large numbers of immigrants. The social efficiency movement grew out of the belief that science could be used to solve these problems. It was led by sociologists and psychologists but was equally embraced by business leaders and politicians.

According to this theory, modern principles of scientific management, intended to maximise the efficiency of factories, could be applied with equal success to schools.

This meant taking Taylor's example of a detailed analysis of the movements performed by expert bricklayers and applying similar analyses to every vocation for which students were being prepared. Then, given the new associationist or connectionist psychology with its emphasis on fundamental building blocks, every step would have to be taught specifically.

Precise standards of measurement were required to ensure that each skill was mastered at the desired level. And because it was not possible to teach every student the skills of every vocation, scientific measures of ability were also needed to predict one's future role in life and thereby determine who was best suited for each endeavor.

For John Bobbitt, a leader in the social efficiency movement, a primary goal of curriculum design was the elimination of waste, and it was wasteful to teach people things they would never use. Bobbitt's most telling principle was that each individual should be educated "according to his capabilities." These views led to a highly differentiated curriculum and a largely utilitarian one that disdained academic subjects for any but college preparatory students.

Thus, scientific management and social efficiency launched two powerful ideas: the need for detailed specifications of objectives and tracking by ability. Although social efficiency began to lose popularity among sociologists and psychologists after the 1930s, these ideas continued to have profound influence on educational practice because they were absorbed in eclectic versions of curricula, such as life adjustment education and work-oriented curriculum, that had strong appeal with school administrators. These ideas contributed to and were buttressed by concomitant developments in psychology and measurement.

IQ Testing

When intelligence tests were brought to the United States in the early 1900s, their interpretation and use were strongly influenced by the eugenics movement and prevalent racist beliefs. Binet, who had developed the first IQ tests in France, believed in "the educability of the intelligence" and deplored the "brutal pessimism" of those who thought it to be a fixed quantity. His program of "mental orthopedics" was intended to improve the use of mental resources and thus help the student become more intelligent than before. In contrast, American psychologists such as Terman, Goddard, and Yerkes promoted IQ test results as a scientifically exact measure of a fixed trait that conformed to the laws of Mendelian genetics.

In a climate of fear about degeneration of the race and the threat of immigration from southern and eastern Europe, most American psychologists emphasised the biological nature of IQ. Goddard referred to intelligence as a "unitary mental process... which is inborn" and "determined by the kind of chromosomes that come together with the union of the germ cells." Terman asserted without evidence his belief in "the relatively greater importance of endowment over training as a determinant of an individual's intellectual rank among his fellows". Both men also pursued the exact ordering of individuals on the scale of IQ, which they believed accounted for moral behavior as well as cognitive performance. Goddard fine-tuned distinctions among the feeble-minded, creating the categories of idiot, imbecile, and moron. Terman saw a precise deterministic relationship between IQ score and lot in life: "an IQ below 70 rarely permits anything better than unskilled labor," "the range of 70-80 is preeminently that of semiskilled labor; from 80-100 that of ordinary clerical labor" and so forth.

Because measured differences were taken to be innate, the only way to cope with inexorable differences in capacity was a highly differentiated curriculum. For example, having attributed the higher rate of "border-line deficiency" scores among "Spanish-Indian, Mexicans in the Southwest, and Negroes" to inherited differences that were most likely racial, Terman urged that "children of this group should be segregated in special classes and be given instruction which is concrete and practical. They cannot master abstractions, but they can often be made efficient workers, able to look out for themselves".

These beliefs and policies were advocated almost 100 years ago, yet they continue to have a profound effect on school practices and public understandings about education. Streaming or tracking by ability began in the 1920s and has continued with only slight diminution in recent decades. As Cronbach explained, the most extreme nativist claims had received widespread attention in the popular press. In contrast, for half a century, more temperate scholarly debates about the fallibility of measures, contributions of environment, and the self-fulfilling consequences of test-based sorting were conducted out of the public eye-until Jensen's work rekindled the controversy.

It was relatively late in the century before scholars or public officials gave attention to the potential harm of labeling children, to the inaccuracy of classifications based on single tests, and to the possible ineffectiveness of special placements. Now at the end of the century, superficially at least, the tide has changed. Most scientists and educated citizens assign a much more limited role to heredity, recognise the multidimensional nature of ability, and are aware of the large effect of past learning opportunities on both test performance and future learning. Herrnstein and Murray's argument-that inherited cognitive differences between races account for apparent differences in life chances-is an obvious carrying forward of earlier ideas but no longer has support in the current scientific community. Such a summary, ignores the persistence of underlying assumptions in popular opinion and cultural norms.

Enduring beliefs about the fixed nature of ability and the need to segregate elite students explain why there is such a conflict in American education between excellence and equity. Although group IQ tests are no longer routinely used to determine children's capabilities, many teachers, policymakers, and lay people implicitly use family background and cultural difference as equally fixed characteristics that account for school failure. The use of readiness measures and achievement tests to categorise students' learning capacity still has the same negative effects as tracking based on IQ, because of the assumption that students in the lower strata should receive a simplified curriculum.

More subtly perhaps, the sorting and classification model of ability testing for purposes of curriculum differentiation has left a legacy that also affects the conception of assessment within classrooms. Even when aptitude measures are replaced by achievement tests, there is still the tendency to use test results to assign students to gross instructional categories rather than having the test tell something particular about what a student knows or how he is thinking about a problem. It is as if achievement is seen as a uni-dimensional continuum and tests are "locator" devices.

Theories of Associationism and Behaviorism

Edward Thorndike's associationism and the behaviorism of Hull, Skinner and Gagne were the dominant learning theories for the greater part of the 20th century. Their views of how learning occurs focused on the most elemental building blocks of knowledge. Thorndike was looking for constituent bonds or connections that would produce desired responses for each situation. Similarly, behaviorists studied the contingencies of reinforcement that would strengthen or weaken stimulus-response associations. The following quotation from Skinner is illustrative:

> The whole process of becoming competent in any field must be divided into a very large number of very small steps, and reinforcement must be contingent upon the accomplishment of each step. This solution to the problem of creating a complex repertoire of behavior also solves the problem of maintaining the behavior in strength.... By making each successive step as small as possible, the frequency of reinforcement can be raised to a maximum, while the possibly aversive consequences of being wrong are reduced to a minimum.

Although it is not possible to give a full account of these theories here, several key assumptions of the behavioristic model had consequences for ensuing conceptualisations of teaching and testing:

1. Learning occurs by accumulating atomised bits of knowledge;
2. Learning is sequential and hierarchical;
3. Transfer is limited to situations with a high degree of similarity;
4. Tests should be used frequently to ensure mastery before proceeding to the next objective;
5. Tests are the direct instantiation of learning goals; and
6. Motivation is externally determined and should be as positive as possible.

Behaviorist beliefs fostered a reductionistic view of curriculum. In order to gain control over each learning step, instructional objectives had to be tightly specified just as the efficiency expert tracked each motion of the brick layer. As explained by Gagne, "to 'know,' to 'understand,' to 'appreciate' are perfectly good words, but they do not yield agreement on the exemplification of tasks. On the other hand, if suitably defined, words such as to 'write,' to 'identify,' to 'list,' do lead to reliable descriptions". Thus, behaviorally-stated objectives became the required elements of both instructional sequences and closely related mastery tests. Although it was the intention of behaviorists that learners would eventually get to more complex levels of thinking, as evidenced by the analysis, synthesis, and evaluation levels of Bloom's Taxonomy, emphasis on stating objectives in behavioral terms tended to constrain the goals of instruction.

Rigid sequencing of learning elements also tended to focus instruction on lowlevel skills, especially for low-achieving students and children in the early grades. Complex learnings were seen as the sum of simpler behaviors. It would be useless and inefficient to go on to ABC problems without first having firmly mastered A and AB objectives. For decades, these principles undergirded each educational innovation: programmed instruction, mastery learning, objectives-based curricula, remedial reading programs, criterion-referenced testing, minimumcompetency testing, and special education interventions. Only later did researchers begin to document the diminished learning opportunities of children assigned to drill-and-practice curricula in various remedial settings.

For all learning theories, the idea of transfer involves generalisation of learning to new situations. Yet because behaviorism was based on the building up of associations in response to a particular stimulus, there was no basis for generalisation unless the new situation was very similar to the original one. Therefore, expectations for transfer were limited; if a response were desired in a new situation, it would have to be taught as an additional learning goal. Cohen, for example, praised the effectiveness of closely aligning tests with instruction, citing a study by Koczor in which students did remarkably better if they were taught to convert from Roman to Arabic numerals and then were tested in that same order. If groups were given "misaligned" tests, however, asking that they translate in reverse order, from Arabic to Roman numerals, the drop-off in performance was startling, from 1.10 to 2.74 standard deviations in different samples. Consistent with the behaviorist perspective, Cohen and Koczor considered Roman-to-Arabic and Arabic-to-Roman conversions to be two separate learning objectives. They were not troubled by lack of transfer from one to the other, nor did they wonder what this implied about students' understanding.

Testing played a central role in behaviorist instructional systems. To avoid learning failures caused by incomplete mastery of prerequisites, testing was needed at the end of each lesson, with reteaching to occur until a high level of proficiency was achieved. In order to serve this diagnostic and prescriptive purpose, test content had to be exactly matched to instructional content by means of the behavioral objective. Because learning components were tightly specified, there was very limited inference or generalisation required to make a connection between test items and learning objectives. Behaviorists worked hard to create a low-inference measurement system so that if students could answer the questions asked, it was proof that they had fully mastered the learning objective.

The belief that tests could be made perfectly congruent with the goals of learning had pervasive effects in the measurement community despite resistance from some. For decades, many measurement specialists believed that achievement tests only required content validity evidence and did not see the need for empirical confirmation that a test measured what was intended. Behavioristic assumptions also explain why, in recent years, advocates of measurement-driven instruction were willing to use test scores themselves to prove that teaching to the test improved learning, while critics insisted on independent measures to verify whether learning gains were real.

Behaviorist viewpoints also have implications for assessment in classrooms. For example, when teachers check on learning by using problems and formats identical to those used for initial instruction, they are operating from the lowinference and limited transfer assumptions of behaviorism. For most teachers, however, these beliefs are not explicit, and, unlike Koczor and Cohen in the example above, most teachers have not had the opportunity to consider directly whether a student "really knows it" if he can solve problems only when posed in a familiar format.

Behaviorism also makes important assumptions about motivation to learn. It assumes that individuals are externally motivated by the pursuit of rewards and avoidance of punishments. In particular, Skinner's interpretation of how reinforcement should be used to structure learning environments had far-reaching effects on education. As expressed in the earlier quotation, it was Skinner's idea that to keep the learner motivated, instruction should be staged to ensure as much success as possible with little or no negative feedback. It is this motivational purpose as much as the componential analysis of tasks that led to the idea of little steps. In Individually Prescribed

Instruction, for example, lessons were designed around skills that the average student could master in a single class period.

Scientific Measurement

It is no coincidence that Edward Thorndike was both the originator of associationist learning theory and the "father" of "scientific measurement" in education. Thorndike and his students fostered the development and dominance of the "objective" test, which has been the single most striking feature of achievement testing in the United States from the beginning of the century to the present day. Recognising the common paternity of the behaviorist learning theory and objective testing helps us to understand the continued intellectual kinship between one-skill-at-a-time test items and instructional practices aimed at mastery of constituent elements.

Borrowing the psychometric technology of IQ tests, objective measures of achievement were pursued with the goal of making the study of education more scientific. According to Ralph Tyler, "The achievement-testing movement provided a new tool by which educational problems could be studied systematically in terms of more objective evidence regarding the effects produced in pupils". Objective tests were also promoted for classroom use as a remedy for embarrassing inconsistencies in teachers' grading practices documented by dozens of research studies.

In one classic study, for example, the same geometry paper was distributed to 116 high school mathematics teachers and received percentage grades ranging from 28 to 92. Many of the arguments made in favor of teacher-developed objective tests suggest issues that are still relevant today. For example, in addition to solving the problem of grader subjectivity, discrete item types also allowed "extensive sampling" and "high reliability per unit of working time". The emphasis on reliability, defined as the consistency with which individuals are ranked, followed naturally from the application to achievement tests of reliability and validity coefficients developed in the context of intelligence testing.

Examples from some of the earliest "standard" tests and objective-type classroom tests are shown in Figure 3. Looking at any collection of tests from early in the century, one is immediately struck by how much the questions emphasise rote recall. To be fair this was not a distortion of subject matter caused by the adoption of objective-item formats. Rather, the various recall, completion, matching, and multiple-choice test types fit closely with what was deemed important to learn in the first part of the century. Nonetheless, once knowledge of curriculum became encapsulated and represented by these types of items, it is reasonable to say that these formats locked-in and perpetuated a particular conception of subject matter.

Present-day calls for assessment reform are intended to counteract the distorting effects of high-stakes accountability tests. Under pressure to improve scores, teachers have not only abandoned untested content but have reshaped their classroom instruction to imitate the format of standardised tests. By hearkening to a day before standardised achievement measures had such serious consequences, reformers seem to imply that there was once a golden era when teachers used more comprehensive and challenging examinations to evaluate student knowledge. A longer-term historical view suggests, however, that the current propensity to focus on low-level skills is merely an exaggeration of practices that have continued without interruption throughout the twentieth century.

The dominance of objective tests in classroom practice has affected more than the form of subject matter knowledge. It has also shaped beliefs about the nature of evidence and principles of fairness. In a recent assessment project, for example, where teachers were nominally seeking alternatives to standardised tests, teachers nonetheless worked from a set of beliefs consistent with traditional principles of scientific measurement. As documented by Bliem and Davinroy, assessment was seen as an official event. To ensure fairness, teachers believed that assessments had to be uniformly administered; therefore, teachers were reluctant to conduct more intensive individualised assessments with only below-grade-level readers.

Because of the belief that assessments had to be targeted to a specific instructional goal, teachers felt more comfortable using two separate assessments for separate goals, a notation system known as "running records" to assess fluency and written summaries to assess comprehension, rather than, say, asking students to retell the gist of a story in conjunction with running records. Most significantly, teachers wanted their assessments to be "objective"; they worried often about the subjectivity involved in making more holistic evaluations of student work and preferred formula-based methods, such as counting miscues, because these techniques were more "impartial."

Any attempt to change the form and purpose of classroom assessment to make it more fundamentally a part of the learning process must acknowledge the power of enduring and hidden beliefs. The present dissonance between instruction and assessment arises because of the misfit between old views of testing and a transformed vision of teaching. However, even reformed versions of instruction have only begun to be implemented. As many studies of teacher change and attempted curriculum reform have documented, all three parts of the old paradigm-social efficiency, behaviorism, and scientific measurement-continue to provide a mutually reinforcing set of ideas that shape current thinking and practice.

Modern Theories of Learning and Assessment

In order to develop a model of classroom assessment that supports teaching and learning according to a constructivist perspective, it is important to see how a reconceptualisation of assessment follows from changes in learning theory and from concomitant changes in epistemology and what it means to know in the disciplines. Figure 2 summarises key ideas in an emergent, constructivist paradigm. According to constructivist theory, knowledge is neither passively received nor mechanically reinforced; instead learning occurs by an active process of sense making. The three-part figure was developed in parallel to the three-part dominant paradigm to highlight respectively changes in curriculum, learning theory, and assessment. In some cases, principles in the new paradigm are direct antitheses of principles in the old paradigm. The interlocking circles again are intended to show the coherence and interrelatedness of these ideas taken together.

The new paradigm is characterised as emergent because it is not fully developed theoretically and surely not adopted in practice. While there are some shared understandings among cognitivists and constructivists about how learning principles should lead to reform of curriculum and instruction, there are also competing versions of these theories and ideas.

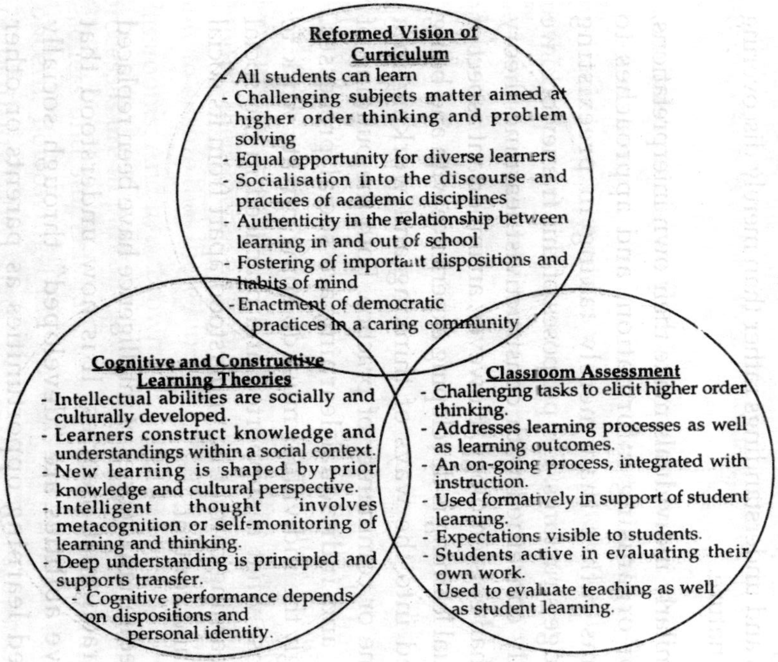

Figure 2. Shared principles of curriculum theories, psychological theories and assessment theory characterizing an emergent, constructivist paradigm

Cognitive and Social-Constructivist Theories

The constructivist paradigm takes its name from the fundamental notion that all human knowledge is constructed. This statement applies both to the construction of public knowledge and modes of inquiry in the disciplines and to the development of cognitive structures in the minds of individual learners. This means that scientists build their theories and understandings rather than merely discovering laws of nature.

Similarly individuals make their own interpretations, ways of organising information, and approaches to problems rather than merely taking in preexisting knowledge structures. For purposes of this framework, we primarily concerned with constructivist learning theory rather than epistemology. However, an important aspect of individual learning is developing experience with and being inducted into the ways of thinking and working in a discipline or community of practice. Both the building of science and individual learning are social processes. Although the individual must do some private work to internalise what is supported and practiced in the social plane, learning cannot be understood apart from its social context and content.

Hereditarian theories of intelligence have been replaced by interactionist theories. It is now understood that cognitive abilities are "developed" through socially mediated learning opportunities as parents or other significant adults interpret and guide children in their interactions with the environment. Interestingly Vygotsky's model of supported learning which has such importance in this volume for the teaching and learning of mathematics, social studies, and so forth, was conceived initially to describe the development of intellectual competence more generally-that is, how one learns to think. Indeed, efforts to study mental processes and how they are developed have blurred the distinctions between learning to think, learning how to solve problems within specific domains and contexts, and developing intelligence. Earlier work in this vein demonstrated the modifiability or instructability of intelligence by working with extreme populations such as educably mentally retarded children and low-functioning adolescents.

More complex, present-day intervention programs by Denny Wolf, Ann Brown, and others can be seen as extensions of this same idea, although improving intelligence per se is no longer the aim. Wolf and Reardon, for example, talk about "developing achievement" by devising a staged curriculum that allows students supported practice with all of the enabling competencies that ensure proficient performance of the final, challenging goals. Wolf and Reardon also note that teachers struggling to create such a curriculum must confront "the fundamental difference between raw aptitude and hard-earned achievement".

Although earlier, Piagetian versions of constructivism focused on individual developmental stages or processes, over time, cognitive psychologists have come increasingly to take seriously the influence of social processes. The rediscovery of Vygotsky provided a theoretical model for understanding how social interactions between adult and child could supply both a model of expertise and the opportunity for guided practice so that the child could eventually internalise desired skills and perform them independently.

According to Vygotsky, the zone of proximal development "is the distance between the actual developmental level as determined by independent problem solving and the level of potential development as determined through problem solving under adult guidance or in collaboration with more capable peers". Bruner's notion of "scaffolding" elaborated on the kinds of social support that would assist a child in performing a task that would otherwise be out of reach; these supports include engaging interest, simplifying the problem, maintaining direction, marking critical features, reducing frustration, and demonstrating.

Other contemporary perspectives go further, suggesting that historical and cultural factors don't merely influence learning but constitute or form identity, images of possible selves, and the repertoire of knowledge and skills needed to participate in a community of practice. A result of this line of thinking, emphasising socially negotiated meaning, has been to complicate the models of effective learning.

In contrast to the decontextualisation and decomposition fostered by associationism, now no aspect of learning can be understood separate from the whole or separate from its social and cultural context. For example, in describing the "thinking curriculum" Resnick and Klopfer emphasised that thinking skills could not be developed independent of content, nor could cognitive skills be separated from motivation. Apprenticeship models are a natural extension of this reasoning because they provide for role development and support for novice performances as well as the contextualisation of skill and knowledge development in a particular community of practice.

For those eager to throw off the shackles of the old paradigm, the role of content knowledge has posed an interesting dilemma. Because mastery of subject matter knowledge has traditionally implied at least some rote memorisation, curriculum reformers have sometimes swung to the other extreme, emphasising processes over content. Yet, it·is a fundamental finding of cognitive research that knowledge enables new learning. Those with existing knowledge stores can reason more profoundly, elaborate as they study, and thereby learn more effectively in that knowledge domain.

Knowledge in a domain includes facts, vocabulary, principles, fundamental relationships, familiar analogies and models, rules of thumb, problem-solving approaches, and schema for knowing when to use what. Effective teaching not only begins by eliciting students' prior knowledge and intuitions, it also develops a community of practice where it is customary for students to review and question what they already believe.

Ironically the validity of efforts to assess prior knowledge are themselves affected by a student's knowledge base and by cultural practices. Often prior knowledge is measured using skills checklists or a pretest version of the intended end-of-unit test. Such procedures are likely to underestimate the relevant knowledge of all but the most sophisticated members of the class since most will not be able to make the translation between pretest vocabulary and their own intuitive knowledge gained in other contexts. Open discussions or conversations are more likely to elicit a more coherent version of students' initial conceptual understandings as well as the reasoning behind their explanations. It is also essential that teachers become familiar with relevant experiences and discourse patterns in diverse communities so that children entering schools will be able to demonstrate their competence rather than appearing deficient because of unfamiliarity with the teacher's mode of questioning.

Adept learners are able to take charge of their own learning using a variety of self-monitoring processes. This concept of metacognition, or thinking about thinking, is a key contribution of the cognitive revolution. Being able to solve problems within each domain of practice involves what Sternberg called "executive processes" such as

(a) recognising the existence of a problem,

(b) deciding on the nature of the problem,

(c) selecting a set of lower-order processes to solve the problem,

(d) developing a strategy to combine these components,

(e) selecting a mental representation of the problem,

(f) allocating one's mental resources,

(g) monitoring one's problem solving as it is happening, and

(h) evaluating problem solving after it is done.

Metacognitive abilities can be learned through socially mediated processes in the same way that first-order cognitive abilities are learned. For example, Brown, Bransford, Ferrara, and Campione conducted studies in which children's comprehension of texts could be improved by teaching them specific strategies such as questioning, clarifying, and summarising-the kinds of strategies that proficient readers use without explicit training. These ideas were then extended to a full-blown reading comprehension intervention, Reciprocal Teaching, which blends the ideas of strategies training and cognitive apprenticeship. Although not a scripted lesson, the routines of reciprocal teaching dialogues give students socially supported practice with four metacognitive strategies-predicting, question generating, summarising, and clarifying-for the purpose of developing a shared understanding of the text. Reciprocal Teaching has been used primarily with learning disabled children and students in remedial reading programs and has shown a median gain of.88 standard deviation for students receiving the intervention compared to controls.

There is a close relationship between truly understanding a concept and being able to transfer knowledge and use it in new situations. In contrast to memorisation-and in contrast to the earlier behaviorist example where students mastered Arabic to Roman numeral translations but couldn't do them in reverse-true understanding is flexible, connected, and generalisable. Not surprisingly, research studies demonstrate that learning is more likely to transfer if students have the opportunity to practice with a variety of applications while learning, and if they are encouraged to attend to general themes or features of problems that imply use of a particular solution strategy. Learning the rules of transfer is, of course, an example of a metacognitive skill that can be supported instructionally.

A goal of teaching should be to help students develop "robust" understandings. The term was prompted by Marilyn Burns's reference to children's understandings as being "fragile"-they appear to know a concept in one context but not to know it when asked in another way or in another setting. Sometimes this fragility occurs because students are still in the process of learning. All too often, however, mastery appears pat and certain but does not transfer because the student has mastered classroom routines and not the underlying concepts. To support generalisation and ensure transfer, that is, to support robust understandings, "good teaching constantly asks about old understandings in new ways, calls for new applications, and draws new connections".

From the situative perspective or the perspective of activity theory the example of children not being able to use their knowledge in new settings might be attributed to their being removed from the original community of practice, which provided both meaning and support for knowledge use. Perhaps. However, a more probable explanation, given the pervasiveness of rote teaching practices, is that children do not really understand even in the initial setting. Although there appears to be disagreement between cognitivists and situativists regarding knowledge generalisation, in fact, both groups of researchers acknowledge the importance of transfer.

Cognitivists focus more on cognitive structures, abstract representations, and generalised principles that enable knowledge use in new situations, whereas "in situativity, generality depends on learning to participate in interactions in ways that succeed over a broad range of situations". Given Vygotsky's explanation that learning occurs on two planes, first on the social plane between people and then within the individual child, it is likely that a successful program of research will need to consider both.

Historically, research on motivation was undertaken by social psychologists separate from the work of learning researchers. Only when cognitive researchers began to study metacognition did they come to realise that students might not employ the strategies they know unless they are motivated to do so.

Traditional classroom practices, especially testing practices, and larger societal norms have created environments in which students may not be motivated to take risks, to try hard, or to demonstrate their intellectual competence. For example, in controlled psychological studies, students are less likely to persist in working on difficult tasks if they know their performance will be evaluated. According to motivational researchers, students who believe that academic achievement is determined by fixed ability are more likely to work toward "performance goals," that is, for grades, to please the teacher, and to appear competent. Lave and Wenger harshly see this "commoditisation of learning" to be a pervasive feature of school settings, where the exchange value of learning outcomes is emphasised over the use value of learning.

According to this stark portrayal, performance-oriented students tend to pick easy tasks and are less likely to persist once they encounter difficulty. Unfortunately, girls are overrepresented in this category. Students who attribute academic success to their own efforts are more likely to adopt "learning goals," which means they are motivated by an increasing sense of mastery and by the desire to become competent. Not surprisingly, students with a learning orientation are more engaged in school work, use more self-regulation and metacognitive strategies, and develop deeper understanding of subject matter.

Social psychological research on achievement motivation has produced a list of evaluation practices that are more likely to foster learning goals and intrinsic motivation. For example, motivation is enhanced if errors and mistakes are treated as a normal part of learning, and if substantive, mastery-based feedback is used rather than normative evaluation. Although most of these laboratorybased recommendations make sense and would contribute to a classroom environment where learning and the development of competence are valued, a few points are worrisome. For example, research on intrinsic motivation urges teachers to "de-emphasise external evaluation, especially for challenging tasks" despite the finding elsewhere that students with a learning orientation "see their teacher as a resource or guide in the learning process, rather than as an evaluator". Moreover, this variable manipulation approach still leaves the teacher responsible for acting on the student in a way that will induce learning.

These findings about the negative effects of evaluation on motivation to learn are the product of the beliefs and practices of the old paradigm, which, following Skinner's formulation, provided extrinsic rewards for success on easy tasks. In such an environment, it is not surprising that so many students have developed a performance rather than a learning orientation. It does not follow, however, that evaluation would always stifle motivation if the culture of the classroom were fundamentally altered, and it is dangerous to conclude on the basis of past studies that somehow students need to be protected from critical feedback.

Evaluative feedback is essential to learning and presumably can be of the greatest benefit when students are tackling problems that are beyond their level of independent mastery. Thus, the idea of withholding evaluation for challenging tasks is contrary to the idea of supporting students' efforts in the zone of proximal development.

Activity theory and Lave and Wenger 's concept of legitimate peripheral participation provide a wholly different view of what might "motivate" students to devote their hearts and minds to learning. According to this theory, learning and development of an identity of mastery occur together as a newcomer becomes increasingly adept at participating in a community of practice. If one's identity is tied to group membership, then it is natural to work to become a more competent and full-fledged member of the group. These ideas come from studying learning in the world outside of school. How is it that children learn their native language from parents and community members without the benefit of formal lessons or memorised rules? How do novices learn how to be tailors or Xerox repair technicians or members of Alcoholics Anonymous? They are not told explicitly how to participate; instead they are provided with opportunities in the context of practice to see, imitate, and try out increasingly complex skills under the guidance of experts and at the same time practice the role of community member.This is again Vygotsky's notion of socially supported learning applied at once to the development of knowledge, cognitive abilities, and identity. Significantly the beginner is also contributing to and affecting the nature of practice shared with old-timers, which also adds to the worth and meaning of effort.

Cognitive apprenticeship programs and Brown and Campione's community of learners are examples of projects in schools aimed at developing communities of practice where students' identities as capable learners are constructed as they participate in active inquiry and discussion of challenging problems.

Modern Vision of Curriculum

The elements of a reformed vision of curriculum, summarised in Figure 2, set the direction for the kinds of changes contemporary educational reformers are trying to make in classrooms. Some of these principles are part of the wider public discourse, familiar to policymakers and journalists as well as educators and researchers; others are articulated by a smaller circle of education reformers.

At the political level, present day educational reform is motivated by the poor performance of students in international comparisons and anxiety about economic competitiveness. In this light, many politicians have accepted the argument from researchers that current problems are in part due to past reforms aimed at minimum competencies and low-level tests. As a result, standards and assessments have been given a central role in reforming public education. The mantra of standards-based reform, "high standards for all students," promises the pursuit of both excellence and equity, goals that were held at odds by prior belief systems. The first set of reform principles-all students can learn, challenging standards aimed at higher order thinking and problem solving, and equal opportunity for diverse learners-are widely shared and recur in legislation, various state and national policy reports, and in standards documents for each of the disciplines.

The remaining elements of the agenda are not so familiar in public arenas but are essential to accomplishing the first set. If it has never been true before, how is it that all students can be expected to master challenging subject matter and perform to high standards unless students can be engaged in learning in fundamentally different ways? Socialisation into the discourse and practices of academic disciplines, authenticity in the relationship between learning in and out of school, fostering of important dispositions and habits of mind, and enactment of democratic values and practices in a community of learners are elements of the reform agenda that follow from the research on cognition and motivation described previously, as well as the basic empirical work that has documented the dreariness and meaninglessness of traditional practice. Taken together they portray the curriculum and classroom environment that would be needed to support student learning at a much higher level.

While not diminishing the significance of these research-based "discoveries," it is important to acknowledge that many of the tenets of reform are not new but bear a remarkable resemblance to ideas advanced by John Dewey 100 years ago. Dewey envisioned a school curriculum that would develop intelligence by engaging students' experience, skills, and interests as the necessary first step in teaching more traditional subject matter. He recognised the social nature of learning and the desirability of creating a miniature community so as to initiate the child into effective social membership. In light of the ambitious claims of the current reforms, it is sobering to recognise how many attempts have been made since then to implement the ideals of progressive education. Successes have been short-lived because, as suggested by Cremin, the complexity of such reforms required "infinitely skilled teachers."

The framework in Figure 2 is intended to address how learning theory and curriculum reform come together at the level of the classroom to reshape instruction and assessment. It would be a mistake, however, to imagine that significant changes could occur in classrooms without corresponding changes in the community and at other levels of the educational and political system. McLaughlin and Talbert, for example, identified the multiple, embedded contexts of teachers and classrooms that may constrain or facilitate educational change. These include subject matter cultures, state and local mandates, the parent community and social class culture, the expectations of teachers in the next higher level of schooling, and professional contexts including teachers' associations and university teacher education programs.

The slogan that "all students can learn" is intended to promulgate what the Malcolm Report called "a new way of thinking." It is a direct refutation of the long-standing belief that innate ability determines life chances. Although such affirmations by themselves will not be sufficient to provide the necessary learning opportunities, the slogan is important because it serves to disrupt the self-fulfilling practices of the old paradigm whereby only certain students were smart enough to master difficult content and therefore only an elite group of students was given access to challenging subject matter.

That the common curriculum should address challenging standards aimed at higher order thinking and problem solving is likewise a rejection of past practices and theory. The transmission model of learning based on rote memorisation of isolated facts removed learning from contexts that could provide both meaning and application. By watering down curricula and emphasising minimum competencies, schools have lowered expectations and limited opportunities to learn. By contrast, if children are presented with more challenging and complex problems and given the support to solve them, they will develop deeper understandings and at the same time become more adept at the modes of inquiry and ways of reasoning that will help them solve new problems in the future.

The commitment to equity as part of standards-based reform implies changing both expectations and resources. Inequality of opportunity pervades the educational system. Not only do children from poor and minority communities receive less rigorous curricula, but they are taught by teachers with less academic preparation and less experience, have access to fewer books and computers, and often attend schools that are unsafe or where it is uncool to take school work seriously.

Equal access to high-quality instruction implies more than even-handed allocation of fiscal and human resources, however. It also requires a more thoughtful and deeper understanding of the tension between treating everyone the same versus respecting and responding to differences. If prior knowledge enables new learning, then it is essential that children from diverse backgrounds have the opportunity to demonstrate what they "know" about a topic and also that they be able to a participate in the classroom in ways that are consistent with the language and interaction patterns of home and community. Brown talks about providing multiple "ways in" to school learning but also insists on "conformity on the basics," everyone must read, write, think, reason, etc. Dewey was often misunderstood as being child-centered at the expense of subject matter. His rejection of this false dualism is equally applicable here. One begins with the experience of the child, but the purpose of the course of study was to bring him into the logically organised and disciplined experience of the mature adult.

Socialisation of Students

If psychological studies have demonstrated that both intelligence and expert reasoning in specific knowledge domains are developed through socially mediated cognitive activity, then there still remains the practical question of how to ensure that these kinds of interactions take place in classrooms. And if, as Brown has suggested, higher thought processes are in part an "internalised dialogue", then how teachers and students talk to each other is of paramount concern. Borrowing from learning in informal settings, sociocultural theorists note that development of competencies normally occurs by experts and novices having the opportunity to converse as they work together on a common goal or product.

The point of "instructional conversations" in school is not just to provide information but to develop shared meanings between teacher and students, to connect schooled concepts to everyday concepts, and to allow students to gain experience with the ways of reasoning and thinking in a field. For example, if in classroom exchanges students are routinely asked to explain their thinking or to clarify terms, then eventually these habits are internalised and become a part of their thinking process as well as a social norm in the classroom.

In mathematics, Schoenfeld discussed the kinds of classroom practices that would foster a "culture of sense making," where "figuring it out" was how students learned to approach mathematical content. The popular writers' workshop satisfies the elements of activity theory in its efforts to support the development of young writers. It provides a model of mature practice, engages students in elements of the process in the context of the whole, and provides the opportunity to try on the role of author.

Whereas the previous principle borrows from models of informal learning in families and communities to change how students learn, this principle suggests that the what of subject matter should also change to provide better connections with the real context of knowledge use. School learning has traditionally between quite distinct from learning outside of school. In-school learning is formal and abstract and removed from the use of tools or contexts that would supply meaning. That's why, for example, students often lose track of the problem they are trying to solve or give silly answers, such as "buses with remainder 3" are needed to take the class to the zoo.

However, school learning is also more reflective, disciplined and general and thereby provides more adaptability to new problem situations than context-specific learning acquired on the job or in the streets. The intention of reformers like Resnick and Newmann is to make the boundaries between school and the world more porous, by bringing authentic contexts into classrooms and at the same time developing habits of inquiry in school that will make students good thinkers and problem solvers in the world.

Once again these ideas were anticipated by Dewey. Dewey did not eschew subject matter or discipline-based study but suggested that students could be inducted into more and more formal knowledge by gaining experience with the practical problems that the disciplines had been developed to solve. His intention in "psychologising" bodies of knowledge, forestalling treatment of them as polished, organised systems, was to connect with children's own understandings and interests and at the same time to reveal the human purposes underlying the disciplines.

Today, Newmann similarly uses authenticity as a key principle of curriculum reform. For Newmann, authentic achievement involves tasks that are significant and meaningful like those undertaken by scientists, musicians, business owners, crafts people, and so forth. Authentic pedagogy is "more likely to motivate and sustain students in the hard work that learning requires" because their intellectual work has meaning and purpose.

Fostering of dispositions and habits

Several of these reform principles, all aimed at changing the nature of classroom interactions as well as curriculum content, are closely interconnected. The goal of fostering important dispositions and habits of minds is largely redundant with the foregoing principles, except that it is worth calling attention to the importance of motivational goals per se. For example, classroom discourse practices that help students develop "a habit of inquiry" not only improve academic achievement in the present but increase the likelihood that students will be motivated to adapt and use their knowledge and skills in new situations.

Not only will they know how to tackle problems, to ask and persist in trying to answer the right questions, to use prior knowledge, to strive for in-depth understanding, and to express their ideas and findings through elaborated communication, but these ways of thinking will have become habits from long practice in a social setting. As suggested earlier, under the learning principle linking motivation and cognitive performance, the goal is not just to motivate students to work hard on challenging problems but to ensure that they develop identities as capable learners.

Enactment of democratic practices

Preparation for democratic citizenship requires more than literacy skills or knowledge about government; it requires providing students from diverse backgrounds the opportunity to learn to live and work together in the world. A number of curriculum theorists and educational reformers have called for a more personalised educational system. Smaller schools, longerterm relationships between teachers and students, and more nurturing roles can clearly be demonstrated to enhance academic learning, but this is not their only purpose.

Joint productive activity around meaningful tasks also develops common understandings and habits of cooperation and mutual respect. Dewey's concept of democracy was based on community, and his intent was to create a miniature society in the school. His interest in bringing practical occupations into schools was to not only to connect with students' understandings but to "cultivate the social spirit" and to "supply the child with motives for working in ways positively useful to the community of which he is a member".

Similarly, Jane Roland Martin argues for a more inclusionary curriculum that emphasises caring, concern, and connection as well as academic knowledge. By engaging students in "integrative activities of living," such as a school newspaper, a theater production, farming, or building an historical museum, students could connect thought to action and gain experience as contributing members of society.

Classroom Assessment

The third circle in the emergent, constructivist framework addresses principles of classroom assessment. What kinds of assessment practices are compatible with and necessary in classrooms guided by social-constructivist views of supported learning? How does assessment fit or intrude, when students are engaged in collaborative conversations and tackle extended real-world problems? If we think of Vygotsky's zone of proximal development, how might assessment insights help extend a student's current level of learning?

The several principles identified in Figure 4 fall into two main categories having to do with transformation of both the substance of assessments and how they are used. First, the substance of classroom assessments must be congruent with important learning goals. In contrast to the reductionistic and decontextualised view of subject matter knowledge produced by the scientific measurement paradigm, this means that the content of assessments must match challenging subject matter standards and be connected to contexts of application. As part of this, assessments must mirror important thinking and learning processes, especially modes of inquiry and discourse, as they are valued and practiced in the classroom.

The purpose of assessment in classrooms must also be changed fundamentally so that it is used to help students learn and to improve instruction rather than being used only to rank students or to certify the end products of learning. The nearly exclusively normative use of tests to compare students to one another and to determine life chances is the key culprit in developing classroom cultures dominated by an exchange value of learning, where students perform to please the teacher or to get good grades rather than to pursue a compelling purpose.

By contrast, in classrooms where participation in learning is motivated by its use value, students and teachers would have a shared understanding that finding out what makes sense and what doesn't is a joint and worthwhile project, essential to taking the next steps in learning. To serve this end, more specific principles of classroom assessment require that expectations and intermediate steps for improvement be made visible to students and that students be actively involved in evaluating their own work.

It goes without saying that such a view of assessment is an ideal, rarely observed in practice. In fact, efforts to pursue this vision of assessment practice must contend with the powerful belief system associated with scientific measurement and the dominant paradigm. To be sure, all of the changes called for by the reform agenda and constructivist theory require new knowledge and profound changes in teaching practices. However, changing assessment practices is the most difficult because of the continued influence of external standardised tests and because most teachers have had little training beyond objective writing and familiarity with traditional item formats to help them know how to assess their students' understandings.

Classroom and External Assessments

Often assessment reform is promoted without distinguishing among several different assessment purposes, yet it is well known that validity depends on how a test is used. A test designed for one purpose may not be valid if used for a different purpose. Should a statewide literacy test administered to third-graders every April for purposes of school accountability and grade-tograde promotion also be used instructionally?

Gipps, speaking from the context of the British educational system, answers, yes, that "assessment for selection, monitoring and accountability can be assessment to support learning." While it is true that something can be learned from every assessment about one's own teaching as well as students' strengths and weaknesses, the uniform nature of external assessments and their infrequency means that they will rarely ask the right questions at the right time to be a part of the ongoing learning process.

The distinction between external and classroom assessment is closely related to the familiar distinction between formative and summative evaluation. Scriven distinguished between the formative role of evaluation feedback, when used internally to improve a program or product, versus the summative role of evaluation data used by outsiders to make final decisions about funding or adopting a program.

Typically, external assessments serve summative purposes such as largescale monitoring of achievement trends, school accountability, school funding, and certification of student proficiency levels. Sometimes external assessments are used formatively at the level of programs, for example, when curriculum revisions are made on the basis of assessment results; but large-scale assessments are rarely used to refocus and improve instruction for individual students. In contrast, classroom assessment should be primarily formative in nature, aimed more at helping students take the next steps in learning than at judging the end points of achievement.

Still, summative evaluation is a natural part of the learning process and should be established as part of classroom routines, especially for older students. Just as students learn the difference between first draft and final versions of their writing, they should also gain experience with making final presentations and reviewing a body of work to reflect on what has been learned. Summative information is also important for reporting to parents and, if done well, classroom assessments can provide more valuable information about student progress than external measures.

External assessments typically dictate uniformity of content and standardisation of procedures, even if they have been reformed to include more open-ended tasks and group problem solving. Standardisation is needed for largescale assessments to ensure that numbers mean the same thing in different contexts, not because of some lingering positivist assumption of pure objectivity but as a basic matter of fairness. For example, if a state assessment is going to be used for school accountability, then content and administration procedures must be standardised to ensure comparability of school results. Everyone takes the same grade-level test at the same, specified time of year. Quite aside from other issues of validity, it would be unfair if some schools were tested in March and others in May, or if some groups had unlimited time to complete the test.

Teachers should not give help during the assessment or restate the questions unless it is part of the standard administration. In contrast, for teaching and learning purposes, the timing of assessments makes the most sense if they occur on an ongoing basis as particular skills and content are being learned. Similarly, the level of the test should be focused closely on the student's current level of functioning even if this means using material that is well above or well below a child's nominal grade level.

In the classroom context, teachers may well provide help while assessing to take advantage of the learning opportunity, to gain insight into a child's thinking, and to see what kinds of help make it possible to take the next steps. Although they are offered as an alternative to standardised procedures, current calls for more interpretive forms of assessment do not obviate the need for external assessments to be consist and generalisable across sites. Moss contrasted traditional psychometric emphases on nomological or generalisable explanation with the goal of the interpretive tradition, which is to understand meaning in context. The interpretive model she proposes, in the context of a teacher licensure assessment, eschews independent ratings of various portfolio components and instead engages pairs of judges in weighing evidence from multiple sources to arrive at a defensible interpretation. This more comprehensive and contextualised look at candidates' performance increases the likelihood of valid assessment results because judges have access to more information. Indeed, they have access, as part of the assessment, to the kinds of corroborating evidence that would normally be gathered as part of traditional validity investigations.

Although judges interpret evidence from various sources rather than using a standard algorithm to combine scores, Moss is nonetheless concerned about whether different pairs of judges will produce consistent results. For example, to ensure adherence to common standards, she finds it necessary to build in review by a "criterion" reader to verify the evidentiary warrant of interpretive summaries and to resolve disagreements between judges.

The degree of consistency required of external assessments will depend on how they are used and whether they rely on precise meanings of scores or less formal assurances of comparability. Linn identifies five different levels of precision in "linking" large-scale assessments, ranging from statistical "equating" to more judgmentally-based "social moderation." For example, a report that National Assessment Reading scores improved by 5 points requires strict equivalence of the assessments from year to year. Professional judgment models that result in accreditation of institutions or passing of degree candidates can rely on less precise correspondence between judgments and standards, but fairness and validity still require that results not depend on the idiosyncrasies of individual judges.

Shepard, Kagan, and Wurtz showed how assessment systems could be designed to serve both external and classroom purposes. However, such multipurpose assessments are costly because the technical and content requirements for each purpose must be satisfied. Although advocates of interpretivist forms of assessment would like to see context and local meanings preserved in what is aggregated for state and national purposes, it is more likely that combining external and classroom purposes will impose standardisation in classrooms.

In Kentucky, for example, all fifth-grade teachers had to use the same mathematics tasks as portfolio entries so that school comparisons could be made. Using instructionally based assessments for accountability purposes also requires standardisation of scoring and external checks, called moderation, to make sure that data being aggregated across classrooms are comparable. The BEAR Assessment System is a rare example of a curriculum embedded, issues-oriented science assessment that was developed to support classroom-level assessment but also satisfies requirements for comparability across classrooms through scoring moderation and a system of link tests.

Because usually a single articulated system cannot be devised, because of cost constraints, or more likely because of local control of curriculum, the model we propose is one of substantive compatibility between two separate assessment systems. Large-scale assessments should be substantively consistent with highquality classroom assessments though procedurally separate; that is, they should be guided by the same curriculum standards, engage students in the same kinds of inquiry and demonstrations of proficiency, and be evaluated in terms of shared criteria for judging high-quality work. Given the extensive evidence that external, high-stakes assessments drive instruction, it is essential that external tests reflect more ambitious conceptions of subject matter knowledge than found in traditional tests; they should also elicit thinking and problem-solving skills.

The recommendation that classroom assessments should operate independently from large-scale, external assessments is based on their needs for quite different types of information: immediate and contextualised data, on the one hand, as opposed to rigorously comparable results, on the other. In addition, the two types of assessments differ sharply in the stringency of technical standards they must meet. External tests must demonstrate higher reliability because they are limited, one-time assessments and are often used to make critically important decisions. In contrast, day-to-day evaluations that are made in the context of classroom lessons do not have such high-stakes consequences for students. If a teacher makes an invalid inference on a given day about a student's understanding, that error can be corrected by new information in subsequent days. The purpose of classroom assessment is not primarily to certify student proficiency levels at a fixed point with precision, but rather to generate hypotheses and guide intervention.

Although single-teacher assessments may be significantly less reliable than formal, external tests, it is nonetheless possible for teachers operating in a systematic way over time to develop highly accurate assessments of student learning.

Assessment Reforms

Assessment reform is part of a larger effort to raise standards and improve the quality of education. Standards-based reform envisions a more challenging curriculum for all students focused on higher order thinking skills and depth of understanding. It involves a thoroughgoing reconceptualisation of what it means to know in each of the disciplines, as well as fundamental changes in teaching and learning consistent with constructivist theory. Transforming assessment is seen as an essential part of curriculum reform because of widespread beliefs and evidence documenting the distorting effects of high-stakes basic skills tests on teaching and learning. This belief, that the content of assessments had to be changed to effect other changes, was captured in the slogan "WYTIWYG," "What You Test Is What You Get."

Assessment reform has played a key role in giving flesh to the intended science reform just as it has in mathematics. Several examples are provided in Figure 5 to illustrate the alignment of assessment with important content and inquiry skills, the use of extended tasks to elicit student reasoning, and the expectation that students be able to communicate their ideas. The character of these tasks and problems is in marked contrast to earlier item types that emphasised knowledge of scientific facts and terminology.

In English language arts and literacy, the same needs for curricular and instructional reforms are felt as in every other field. If anything, the hostility toward traditional standardised measures has been even greater in this subject area than in others because of the serious ways that tests have misrepresented children's skill development. For example, in their review of formal early literacy tests Stallman and Pearson document that most measures are based on outmoded theories of early reading development. In fact, readiness tests and first-grade reading tests look very similar to those designed by Gates and Bond in the 1930s.

Moreover, such tests engage young children in a set of activities that are anathema to highquality reading instruction. Skills are tested out of context, items require that students recognise answers rather than produce an oral or written response, and the activity is dominated by test-taking behavior such as keeping the right place and bubbling answers rather than reading for meaning. The complaints against writing tests are even more severe. Typically, writing tests measure grammar, spelling, and punctuation skills but not the ability to write. When writing tests include an essay component, they still lack the properties of authentic writing situations. The reason for writing is artificial and often unmotivating, the assigned topic may be unfamiliar, the absence of resources such as books and peers is inauthentic, timing constraints are unlike the usual time allotted to develop a piece of writing, and lack of opportunity to revise and edit is inconsistent with good writing practice. Perhaps it is because existing measures were so at odds with the substance of good instruction, that literacy experts have gone to the greatest lengths to revise the form of assessment as well as its content.

Assessment Tools

A broader range of assessment tools is needed to capture important learning goals and to more directly connect assessment to ongoing instruction. As illustrated above, the most obvious reform has been to devise more open-ended performance tasks to ensure that students are able to reason critically, to solve complex problems, and to apply their knowledge in real-world contexts. In addition, if instructional goals include developing students' metacognitive abilities, fostering important dispositions, and socialising students into the discourse and practices of academic disciplines, then it is essential that classroom routines and accompanying assessments reflect these goals as well.

Furthermore, if assessment insights are to be used to move learning along rather than merely to keep score on how much learning has occurred so far, then assessment has to occur in the middle of instruction, not just at end points, and must focus on processes of learning-what strategies are children using-not just outcomes. In response to these needs, the armamentarium for data gathering has been expanded to include observations, clinical interviews, reflective journals, oral presentations, work samples, projects, and portfolios.

Alternative Forms of Assessment

There are several of the more prominent alternative forms of assessment. Performance assessments are not considered as a separate category because performance tasks are expected to be a part of ongoing instructional activities and therefore are included in observation-based assessments; they are among the entries in a portfolio assessment system, as well as being used in on-demand, formal tests.

External assessments are necessarily structured and formal to ensure comparability across school settings. Within classrooms, however, it is possible to use both formal and informal assessments, with the balance between the two shifting across the age span. For very young children, assessments should be almost entirely informal. For example, parents and teachers use observations and work samples to know when scribbling has progressed enough and letter recognition is in place so that demonstration of specific letter shapes would be appropriate.

As children grow, it is not only possible for them to participate in more formal events, designated for assessment purposes, but desirable that they do so, if such events are authentic and consistent with the goal of inducting students into the practices of the discipline. For example, middle-school students might make presentations to report findings from a field project or take a performance-based examination to see if they can use inquiry skills to help conceptualise the class's next project.

Observation-based assessment tools used in early literacy classrooms illustrate how data about learning can be collected systematically alongside of normal instructional activities. For example, "running records" developed by Marie Clay are a notation system used during oral reading to keep track of a child's omissions, substitutions, and self-corrected miscues. By close attention to the nature of student errors-called "miscues" to emphasise that students are responding to cues even when mistaken-teachers can identify students' word recognition skills as well as their ability to make sense of the text.

To assess comprehension, teachers might also use story retellings or ask specific questions about the text. Used routinely as a follow-up to reading activity, such assessments provide valuable information but also convey to students the importance of thinking and talking about what they read.

Brief assessments during reading time can be used to make immediate instructional decisions, such as focusing on compound words, emphasising sense making, or changing text level; but informal assessment techniques can also be structured to document children's growth over time, especially if running records and story retells are recorded in relation to graded texts or reading passages of increasing difficulty.

Consistent with the idea of socialising students into the discourse and practices of a literacy community, Mervar and Hiebert documented that children's abilities to choose books can be developed as a goal of instruction and correspondingly are amenable to systematic observation. For example, they noted that students without previous modeling by adults might pick a book without opening it, whereas children in a literature-based classroom were more likely to sample a number of books before choosing by reading segments aloud or looking for specific topics.

Clinical interviews or think-alouds are research techniques that can also be used in classrooms to gain insights about students' learning. One-on-one interactions provide a more extended opportunity to hear and observe students' strategies and to have them explain their reasoning. Individual interviews also make it possible to conduct "dynamic assessments" that test what a student can do with adult support. In these interactions a teacher-clinician is not merely collecting data but is gathering information and acting on it at the same time, thus completely blurring the boundaries between assessment and instruction.

Portfolios are another, highly popularised, new form of assessment. Borrowing from the arts and from professions such as architecture and advertising where individuals collect samples of their best work to demonstrate their talents and skills, the intention of assessment reformers is to use portfolios of student work to provide more authentic documentation of achievement. When considered from the perspective of external, accountability assessments, portfolio-based assessments face a number of serious obstacles including reliability of scoring and fairness questions such as "Whose work is it, really?"

However, when used in classrooms solely for teaching and learning purposes, portfolios can provide an organising structure for teacher-student critiques and student self-reflections, thereby fostering metacognitive goals that might not be attended to if the various assignments in the portfolio were undertaken separately. Within classrooms the relevant comparison is not whether portfolio assessments can be made as reliable and rigorously comparable as standardised measures but whether a portfolio structure can help teachers and students become more systematic in analysing and learning from student work than would ordinarily occur as a part of instructional activities.

A number of researchers have written about the unique features of portfolios as a teaching tool. Yancey, for example, argues that reflection is the defining characteristic of writing portfolios. Through construction of portfolios students set goals for learning, review their work and develop criteria for selecting particular pieces over others, learn to evaluate the strengths and weaknesses of their own work, and gain experience in communicating their purposes and judgments to others. Work by Camp and Hilgers among others illustrates that students can develop the ability to articulate and apply critical criteria if they are given practice and experience doing so.

Klimenkov and LaPick, teachers at Orion Elementary School, combined the use of portfolios with student-led conferences. Their goals included student empowerment as well as helping students understand what steps they needed to take to move ahead. Evaluation of the Orion project found that students indeed took greater responsibility for their own learning; but the drop-off in effort after the midyear conference suggested that the device still relied on external motivation to a large extent. Duschl and Gitomer sought to create what they call a portfolio culture in classrooms by using portfolio assignments and negotiated criteria to engage in "assessment conversations." Through such conversations teachers find out what students know, students gain experience with processes of scientific explanation, argument, and presentation, and students learn to apply standards of scientific plausibility. Portfolios are the vehicle for conceptualising and structuring these classroom interactions. Whether portfolios can be used for both classroom and external purposes is highly controversial.

Large-scale assessment purposes bring with them the need for uniform assignments and scoring criteria. Not only will such constraints make it less likely that instructional activities will fit the learning needs of individual students, but the high-stakes, evaluative context may also defeat efforts to engage students in taking responsibility for their own learning. While acknowledging the tension, Au and Valencia argued that the benefit teachers derived from learning to score portfolios and the improvement in students' writing proficiency, even from a mandated portfolio system, were sufficient to warrant their use. Myers suggested that there might be a conscious interaction between portfolios constructed for formative and summative purposes rather than assuming that a single portfolio could reasonably serve both purposes.

While we think it will be impractical to implement two fullblown portfolio systems in the same subject area throughout the school year, it would be feasible for classroom portfolios to include evidence from other forms of external assessments, such as on-demand performance tasks or standardised tests, and to address explicitly their relationship to classroom-based evidence. As a general rule, teachers should use a variety of assessment tools, choosing in each case the mode of data collection that best captures intended knowledge and skills in their context of use. Sometimes this will mean using more traditionallooking quizzes and examinations.

As is the case for all assessment modes, there should be an explicit rationale for using conventional assessment techniques both with respect to the format of test questions and for the "on-demand" character of test events. Essay questions, for example, may still be the best means for students to demonstrate their ability to use either historical or scientific evidence to support an argument. Traditional fill-in-the-blank, short-answer, or multiple-choice questions may also be useful in checking for certain kinds of procedural knowledge, so long as these skills are represented in proportion to their substantive importance in the curriculum and not simply because they are the easiest to measure.

Learning goals should also determine whether and in what proportion assessments should be administered "on demand." This point is often in contention for both teacher education and doctoral students. "If you believe in assessment reform, why give tests or doctoral comprehensive examinations?" The answer should be that classroom participation, extended projects, research papers, and tests each support and reflect different kinds of learning and therefore provide different kinds of evaluation data.

Assuming that content has been reformed in the ways described previously, tests demonstrate "walking around knowledge," that is, the conceptual schemes and big ideas that you should have in your head without having to look them up in a book or ask a colleague. For prospective teachers, this means that formal examinations should tap the kinds of knowledge required "on demand" in authentic applications, for example, when asked for your teaching philosophy in a job interview, when making an instructional decision on the fly, when arguing for one choice over another in a district curriculum committee meeting, or when explaining student work and assessment data to a parent.

Similarly, for doctoral students, tests can be an authentic measure of professional knowledge if they draw on the expertise one needs to answer questions from school board members, to review manuscripts submitted to journals, to brainstorm about study designs, to respond off the cuff in a professional debate, and so forth.

Multiple Modes of Assessment

Variety in assessment techniques is a virtue, not just because different learning goals are amenable to assessment by different devices, but because the mode of assessment interacts in complex ways with the very nature of what is being assessed. For example, the ability to retell a story after reading it might be fundamentally a different learning construct than being able to answer comprehension questions about the story; both might be important instructionally. Therefore, even for the same learning objective, there are compelling reasons to assess in more than one way, both to ensure sound measurement and to support development of flexible and robust understandings.

In the measurement literature, it is well know that assessment formats can have significant effects on performance levels. For example, one of the best known and pervasive effects is the relative advantage of women over men on essay examinations compared to multiple-choice measures of the same content domain. In science, Shavelson, Baxter, and Pine found that students did not score equivalently on paper-and-pencil, computer simulations, or hands-on versions of the same electric circuit problems. In the Orion portfolio project described previously, teachers worried that students who were shy or suffering from stage fright were at a disadvantage in demonstrating their knowledge in student-led conferences. When different results occur from different assessment formats, it will depend on the situation whether one result should be treated as more valid than the others.

Validity studies of male-female differences on Advanced Placement history exams, for example, suggest that multiple-choice and essay exams are actually measuring different constructs roughly corresponding to historical knowledge and historical argument. Instead of concluding that one format is biased, the evidence suggests that both formats are needed to adequately represent the content domain. By contrast, in the accommodations literature, certain test formats would be deemed biased if irrelevant features of the assessment prevent students from demonstrating their true level of competence. This occurs, for example, when English language proficiency is confounded with assessment of mathematics or when learning disabled students are unable to demonstrate their knowledge because of excessive writing demands or lengthy examination periods. In the case of nonconstant results for tasks believed to be equivalent, when there is no basis for choosing between bias or multipleconstruct interpretations, as in the Shavelson example above, the best strategy is to use multiple data sources for purposes of triangulation without presuming that one assessment mode is more accurate than others.

From the perspective of assessment fairness in classrooms, students should be allowed to demonstrate their competence using the particular conditions that show them to best advantage. This might mean giving an oral presentation rather than taking a written exam, writing about a topic that is familiar, having access to translated versions of the task, and so forth. From a teaching perspective, however, students should not always rely on the format that is most comfortable. Good instruction focuses on areas of weakness as well as strengths and ensures that students' knowledge becomes increasingly flexible and robust across contexts of application. To do this, teachers must be aware of how variation in assessment or instructional task features affects performance.

3

Teachers and Diversity Issues

Good teachers not only convey a body of knowledge to their students, but they are also aware of how to convey that knowledge by connecting their own experience with their students' experience of the world. Aspects of a teacher's personal identity are important as the teacher tries to relate to students and instill in them an interest in a field. A teacher's learning and teaching styles are one important part of diversity. How such styles match with students' learning styles can play an important part in the success of any course.

When we speak of diversity in the classroom, we usually focus on the diversity of the students in the room. We often forget that the teacher also brings a range of diversity issues to the classroom. Every teacher brings his or her physical appearance and culture into the room at the same time as the students do. How you look, how you speak, how you act upon your opinions of the role of academics, and the extent to which these differ from the physical, cultural and intellectual backgrounds of your students will have a profound effect on the interactions in your classroom. Thus you need to be aware of possible reactions among the students to your race, gender, age, ethnicity, physical attributes and abilities. Preparing for such reactions will involve not only knowing as much as you can about your students, but also turning the mirror to yourself, and finding out more about your own diversity issues.

Dealing wth Diversity in Classroom

Teachers should be aware of the comfort level they have in discussing these topics before they enter a classroom. It is crucial to understand how you feel about these issues and what you would say in a room where some may not understand your particular position. If diversity becomes a topic of discussion in the class, students will expect the teacher to be able to explain his or her perspective. Try to have thought of a formulation that clarifies your perspective, while leaving enough room for your students' perspectives in the discussion. You may look like you "belong to" a minority, or to the majority, even if you do not. Either way, your students will initially perceive this to the exclusion of your own diverse experiences, intentions, background, etc. until they get to know you better.

Students who perceive the teacher as belonging to a particular racial or ethnic group and who then draw initial conclusions from that classification can affect the class atmosphere either negatively or positively from the first day. It is probably impossible to determine exactly to what extent perceptions of race, gender and ethnicity motivate such challenges to the authority of the professor. Clearly however, such perceptions do color people's everyday assumptions.

Some students can see a professor's gender and ethnic diversity as advantages. If a student does repeatedly challenge the teacher in a manner the teacher deems inappropriate, however, it may be wise to ask the student privately to come to an office hour. There the teacher can discuss the possible reasons behind the student's behavior in a non-threatening and less public place. Discussing the problem privately may avoid the possibility of a single studentteacher relationship affecting the tenor of the entire class. It will also give the student the chance to explain his or her position, thus giving the student a hearing which may in itself defuse the situation. Showing the student that you care about his or her progress, all the while maintaining your professional demeanor will make the point that you both have a professional teacher/student relationship to uphold. Listening to the student, and being willing to advise him or her in a friendly manner will emphasise that relationship.

The best way to minimise the likelihood that your own perceived diversity will affect student behavior is to establish a "safe" environment in which the class can discuss both your and your students' diversity. Such a safe atmosphere establishes the difference between a highly successful class, and one where both teacher and students fear one another, experiencing discomfort when it comes to discussing the "real" issues. This fear can be the fear of being labeled as an outsider, or the fear of offending someone and making him or her feel unwanted in the group. Either way, fear is not a good basis on which to start any discussion.

The issue of diversity will be an important point of interest to the students you meet in your classrooms because the average 18-22 year-old student is in a stage of development where cultural and value orientation is being established. For the first time, these students find themselves in an environment where they must form opinions on these topics without worrying about what their elders will say. For many of them, the school is the first place where they meet a wide range of people from various groups and where they leave their habitual groups behind. The school environment gives them a chance to explore these issues, and most students react well when they have the chance to reevaluate the opinions with which they grew up, and to develop themselves independently.

In addition to such visible differences as race, gender, and physical attributes, any teacher also brings invisible diversity to the classroom. Invisible differences such as political opinion, sexual orientation, ethnicity when it is separate from distinct racial characteristics, teaching and learning styles, regionalism, class, family history, and religion have more to do with an individual's own self-perceptions and definitions than with others' immediate perceptions. These internal perspectives influence how a person sees the world, and are a source of personal identity. All people are shaped by a complex mix of experiences, backgrounds, as well as their visible identity. Everyone in a classroom is struggling with the tension between group identity and the feeling of individual worth that transcends the group.

The assumption that diversity has only to do with the students in the classroom can make it hard for a teacher to recognise personal hidden assumptions. This may in turn hinder proper learning in class, as a teacher may unwittingly slant the choice of reading materials or the direction and form of class discussions. Of course, any choice of class materials presupposes an exclusion of other materials; any organisation of those materials into a coherent syllabus involves decisions about which elements to emphasise. These devices are necessary for structuring any class and most often benefit from the teacher's perspective. As long as you are aware of your own presuppositions and assumptions, however, you can avoid the kinds of slant in your class that can be harmful to students, or unnecessarily strain your relations with them.

The diversity in your classroom can serve as a catalyst for intellectual and emotional growth, both for you and for your students. Seen as an opportunity rather than as a handicap, the diversity of your class can facilitate the kinds of change that a university education is designed to promote. A motivated teacher can challenge hidden assumptions in the classroom, and provide equal and fair access for students from all walks of life to his or her chosen field. As students graduate and begin work in their professions they may carry the enthusiasm and openness they have experienced in academia out into society.

Teacher assistants (TA) who go directly into graduate school and immediately start teaching are less likely to have problems relating to their students' culture than older teachers. Younger TAs are close enough in age to have been exposed to similar television shows, music, political events and so forth. However, many young TAs fear that they will fail to command attention and respect because they are too close to their students' age. This fear usually subsides rather quickly when it becomes clear that most students respect their teachers, young or older, as long as the teachers come to class wellprepared. TAs are considerably more knowledgeable in their field than most undergraduates, and will have little trouble commanding student respect if they prepare well for class and behave respectfully toward students.

Many professors and TAs who are four or more years older than their students, however, often experience a mini-generation gap. They no longer share the same tastes in music or in clothing and they watch differenttelevision shows. Often, older teachers have considerably different views on politics and current culture than their students simply because they grew up at a different time. Such differences are not negligible. One runs the risk of seeming so old-fashioned and out-of-touch that the topic one is presenting seems "purely academic" to the students. Such attitudes arise more often in courses that meet general undergraduate requirements, since students have not chosen those courses out of personal interest in the topic.

You can more easily engage your students if you can speak to them about their culture and put the major topics of your field into the context of their lives. Here you might take the opportunity to become a student of your students by educating yourself about their experience of the world. Some knowledge of current popular culture will be a step towards learning about the students' interests. Such familiarity with their interests can mean the difference between being able to teach and interest students in your field, or presenting them with material that seems irrelevant.

If you have a relatively small class (20 to 25) one very effective way to learn about your students is to schedule two required office hours for each student, one at the beginning of the class and one at the end. All students then feel as if you know them and respect them individually. Minority students in particular feel more included if they have the opportunity to speak to you personally, and they are then more likely to participate actively for the rest of the semester.

Teaching and Learning Styles

Learning Styles

In recent decades, studies have shown that students have varying learning styles, and that no single teaching style fulfills all students' needs. Learning styles have very little to do with the student's motivation or attitude toward the class or the material. Often, professors and TAs complain that some students do not apply themselves to their studies, and therefore do not learn well. However, it may be that the teacher simply has not yet addressed these students' particular needs in class, and that new approaches will reach the students more effectively. A student's learning style has to do with the way he or she processes information in order to learn it and then apply it.

Some students may be visual learners, and prefer to study graphs, look at models and pictures, and take notes to review later. Such students react well to extensive blackboard use, and handouts with appropriate illustrations. Others are aural learners-they listen closely in class, often read out loud when studying or subvocalise during lectures in class, and find it helpful to confer with their peers in class to confirm information. These students work well in study groups where discussion of the material reinforces class discussion and lectures. They may also react well to tapes and films in class.

Verbal learners are likely to absorb reading materials and lectures more easily than other students. They seem to learn best from written materials, rather than from visual materials such as graphs and illustrations. Most teachers are verbal learners, and thus find it easiest to relate to and teach such students.

Still others may be sensing learners. Such students may be tactile learners who favor subjects that allow them to work with their hands. These students learn best by handling the textures and shapes of objects as they apply their knowledge: they enjoy looking at and handling objects of interest to the topic, such as original documents, photos, magazines, natural objects etc. Or sensing learners may be kinesthetic learners who learn and remember by moving around physically. Moving them into small groups or pairs for discussion, having them participate actively in an experiment, or getting them to "act out" a debate by placing them on opposite sides of the room will help this type of student to remember the content of the discussion.

Both tactile and kinesthetic learners prefer "real-life" connections to the topic, rather than theoretical approaches. They are "active learners" who learn best by physically doing things, rather than reflecting about them by themselves, and thus they react well to group work. They may also often learn by induction rather than deduction.

Inductive learners prefer to begin with experience or hard data, and infer the principles behind them. Deductive learners prefer to start with abstractions or principles, and enjoy deducing the consequences. Most college classes are taught in a deductive manner, not only because it is easier and less time-consuming to teach a class this way, but also because most often the teachers themselves are deductive learners. Deductive learners may often be reflective learners who prefer to think about the topic by themselves, or at most in pairs, and to work out the solutions. They do not react as well as others to group work.

These different learning styles explain why in most classes, the student evaluations show that some students see group work as the most important part of their learning experience, while others from the same class complain that they dislike group work and find it unhelpful. Providing a variety of approaches to the material can keep most of the students engaged in the class throughout the semester.

Global learners seem more likely than others to see a project as a whole and have trouble breaking it down into its component parts. Teachers who expect them to start analysis from abstract concepts in order to reach a conclusion may find themselves as frustrated with the result as the students. Abstractions may be difficult for this kind of learner, because they grasp information in large chunks and have a hard time analysing a topic from incomplete information. This type of student is excellent at synthesis, and by the end of a class may even outpace his or her peers in coming to appropriate conclusions quickly, but he or she often has trouble understanding material when first faced with a variety of pieces of information that make an incomplete picture.

Sequential learners, on the other hand, are good at analysis of concepts because they learn linearly. When doing a project, they can take partial information and organise it into a logical order, and they can see what must be done first, next and last. They are patient with the fact that a typical class gives them information in a certain order, and that they must wait until the end of the semester to get the full picture the teacher is trying to present. Since most classes are organised sequentially, this kind of learner excels in the typical college class.

No teacher can make all students happy all the time, partly because of the diversity of learning styles in any class, and partly because each person uses a particular mix of the learning styles discussed above. No student is 100% a global learner or 100% a tactile learner. Preference for one style or another may be strong, moderate, or balanced. However, it is important is to recognise that learning styles differ, and that your students may not learn well if you use only your style. In order to teach everyone most effectively, a teacher cannot consistently ignore a whole sector of the class simply because their learning styles do not correspond to the teacher's preferred teaching habits. To reach as many students as possible, the teacher must incorporate varying teaching techniques and strategies into the classroom. Lectures may be appropriate for verbal and aural learners, group work may be appropriate for kinesthetic learners, but any teaching style to the exclusion of the others will also exclude those students who do not learn best by that style.

A student's learning style may be defined in part by the answers to five questions:

1. What type of information does the student preferentially perceive:
   - sensory – sights, sounds, physical sensations, or
   - intuitive – memories, ideas, insights?
2. Through which modality is sensory information most effectively perceived:
   - visual – pictures, diagrams, graphs, demonstrations, or
   - verbal – sounds, written and spoken words and formulas?
3. With which organization of information is the student most comfortable:
   - inductive – facts and observations are given, underlying principles are inferred, or
   - deductive – principles are given, consequences and applications are

   deduced?
4. How does the student prefer to process information:
   - actively – through engagement in physical activity or discussion, or
   - reflectively – through introspection?

5. How does the student progress toward understanding:
   - sequentially – in a logical progression of small incremental steps, or
   - globally – in large jumps, holistically?

Such questions will provide the basis for choosing a balance of teaching methods and techniques that are the most effective. Any teacher must eventually decide which mix works best for the subject matter and for the kinds of students in a class. The questions themselves suggest that a teacher should begin with a variety of approaches, and, after deciding which are the most effective for the students, select techniques to add to his or her repertoire.

Teaching Styles

As students' learning styles vary, and a teacher might have a complex mixture in a single class. However, the average college teacher is much more likely to be sequential, verbal, deductive, and reflective than his or her students. Traditionally, college teachers prefer to organise their class in a "logical" order during the semester, starting with simple premises and working up to a more complex view of the field in question. They use lectures and discussions as the primary means of transmitting information to the students, and classes are usually conducted in a deductive manner, with principles clearly laid out and the expectation that the students can draw consequences and come up with applications.

Students are encouraged to work individually, and achievement is measured by their ability to produce "original" materials or answers. Instructors generally emphasise individual accomplishment, verbal assertiveness in class discussion and competition for grades among students instead of collaboration. As a matter of fact, the academic community often discourages or even punishes collaboration, because it fears a heightened potential for plagiarism in a collaborative effort. Such a teaching method encourages learners who already share the teacher's learning style, but it slows down learners who must adapt to conditions of learning that do not come naturally to them.

Thus a dominant "academic culture" exists in college classrooms which encourages sequential, verbal, deductive and reflective learners to progress quickly to advanced positions in a field. This leaves behind equally intelligent and resourceful students who must wonder if there is a place for them to excel in the academic world.

Academic Culture and Reacculturation

In the above discussion the terms "academic culture" and "academic community" were used to describe what students encounter when they come into the school. These terms were chosen because they are particularly apt for what happens in school classrooms. Students arriving on campus must, in a sense, learn a new language and new rules of conduct to fit in with the expectations of professors and other students who have already had school experiences. The university classroom has norms and values which may be foreign to first generation university goers, or to students from a cultural minority.

University classroom culture values verbal assertiveness in discussions, active participation on an individual level in class, and competition among students for marks of excellence. Teachers prefer a certain form of self expression or style of speech: it should be rational, logical, and derive consequences from general principles. Styles of speech emphasising personal experience and emotion or using vernacular dialects are not encouraged, and may even count against students when it comes time to grade them. A certain classroom decorum is expected: students are expected to come to class dressed in what is conceived of as "an appropriate style". Students are to follow rules of conduct in discussion which underline the teacher's power to direct and control the class and they must make and maintain eye contact with the teacher as they contribute to the discussion. A mix of lecturing and the Socratic method of questioning students in class dominates teaching styles. Verbal learning is assumed and deductive logic remains the dominant format. The fact that students must master this complex "grammar" of the university classroom to make passing marks means that all students coming to the university must be reacculturated.

Reacculturation is thus not only an issue for "minorities"-but is also important for any student who is the first family member to arrive at the university. First generation university students are disadvantaged because the academic culture is not a tradition in their family history, nor have they encountered it among their friends. Other "minority" cultures simply underline the problem most clearly because they often do not have the academic culture in their backgrounds. In addition, many minority cultures may even value things that are antithetical to the academic culture.

The university classroom experience may be doubly difficult for cultures that do not value individual success over group results, or that value modesty over individual assertiveness. Hispanics, Native Americans and Asian Americans, for example, come from cultures that do not traditionally condone the behavior expected of university students in class. In all three cases, direct eye contact, maintained for even a minimum of time, may be considered highly impolite, especially toward such figures of respect as teachers.

Asserting oneself in discussion may seem to them dangerously close to challenging the teacher and may imply that the teacher does not have the authority or the knowledge to conduct the class adequately. These groups often view standing out among one's fellows in a competitive manner as damaging to the peer group. These students may view the Anglo emphasis on "leadership qualities" as destructive and self-serving, while their teachers may admire such qualities in their students.

The predominant academic teaching style at universities is thus really an unexamined cultural stance that involves complicated rules of conduct and its own language. This cultural norm is often foisted onto students under the guise of academic standards. Of course, academic standards are important, and should be to any teacher. The point here is that any single teaching style to the exclusion of others does not necessarily ensure any standards. It simply means that teachers may be leaving behind certain students who could be learning "up to standard" expected.

Collaborative Learning

A culture is based on a social and a linguistic community. Reacculturation in the first years of a university education teaches students the kind of language and behaviors necessary to be successful in the university world and in many professional situations beyond. Students coming to the university for the first time, or even just starting a new class each semester, must find their place in a new group in which they must become members. Learning the "language" of their new group and understanding its rules will enable them to perform adequately and provide them with a passport to other groups. Kenneth A. Bruffee in Collaborative Learning: Higher Education, Interdependence and the Authority of Knowledge suggests that this reacculturation happens most quickly and successfully for students when they work together with the other members of the class, rather than concentrating on solitary work.

People in all fields make advances through collaborative learning, learning which happens through interdependent work with others. Literary critics, chemists, lawyers, historians or journalists, the knowledge these people have of their chosen field is socially constructed, and has been arrived at through conversations among peers. Advances in the science community, among historians, and among literary critics are announced through published papers which are then discussed publicly in journals and at conferences. Writing, another form of discussion or conversation, airs a certain theory which the community either accepts or rejects. Knowledge is constructed interdependently by people who talk together and reach a consensus.

Since such a "conversation among peers" is necessary for establishing criteria and learning new facts in every arena of human learning, Bruffe suggests that the most effective way to learn-and thus to teach-is to incorporate collaborative strategies into the university classroom. In addition to the traditional lecture, structured small group discussions can be very useful to expose students of all learning styles and backgrounds to a new discipline. The teacher can divide classes into smaller groups who must each work toward a consensus on a specific problem. Then the teacher can conduct a whole-class discussion of the groups' results, with an eye toward creating class consensus, but also taking into account those places where groups could not reach a consensus. This classroom strategy teaches the kinds of activities and skills that students will later need to use in their chosen fields. The questions will remain the same, be they questions in a class or, later, questions that the young scientist or literature teacher must answer:

- Here are different results: why and how are they different?
- How did we get the results?
- What was the situation?
- What were the assumptions?
- What was the process?
- Can the differences be "explained" in terms of the rules we already know?
- Can the differences be reconciled?
- How do we-or do we-change the rules so that the differences will no longer challenge accepted rules and practices?

Creating a classroom where students participate actively in such questions not only trains students for their future careers, but also makes them learn the current material more solidly because it engages them more completely and it teaches them about negotiating within a diverse community. When the teacher attaches the actual class topic and material to the success of the class as a community, he or she puts each student in the position of establishing an important role for him or herself in that community and this gives each student responsibility for the success of the class.

Small group activities release the students from the fear of speaking out in front of an entire class, or of being directly judged by the teacher all the time, while putting them in the limelight in a smaller setting, where participation counts even more because there are fewer people involved. Engaging students actively makes it possible for them to learn the rules (and thereby join a new community of knowledge) because they have to use those rules to solve the problems given in class. Such exercises encourage students to think independently at the same time as they work interdependently in an academic field. In a small group, students must find a way to balance their earlier knowledge of the world with the new rules they are learning. They must also deal with their peers' preconceptions and prejudices that stem from their own particular experience and background. In group discussion, those peers become real to them in ways they cannot during a lecture where the teacher is the focus of attention. Active participation in group work forces face-to-face encounters that do not allow for abstract preconceptions about other class members.

Inclusive Teaching Strategies

Teaching to the Individual Student

The teacher who tries to be sensitive to all of these diverse student issues may, understandably, feel overwhelmed at having to do something about all of them right away. The fear of unintentionally alienating a student by a slip of the tongue can cause stress to any well-meaning teacher. It is important to keep in mind that developing a coherent teaching strategy to reach diverse students takes time. Try not to refashion your entire classroom style at once. It is often most effective to concentrate one particular aspect at a time. Add new techniques or strategies incrementally, and get used to how they work before introducing additional ones.

The most important thing to keep in mind is that teaching for diversity means teaching to the individual. By taking an interest in students' experiences, interests, beliefs, and goals, you take the most important step in making students feel that they can succeed in college. In addition, recognise that differences between individuals are more significant than differences between groups. The greatest challenge you face as a teacher is not tailoring your teaching to be sensitive to a whole group, but rather tailoring your teaching in a way that will meet the diverse learning styles of each student.

Some students, regardless of race or gender, find the university an impersonal environment that does not connect to their own experiences and goals. There are also students who lack confidence or assertiveness, yet are quite capable of learning the content and skills of the courses they take. Academics generally perceive verbally aggressive students as being brighter. But some students simply have been raised in environments where they have not been encouraged to speak out. In addition, feelings that the university lacks relevance to their lives or treats them as anonymous faces may add an extra burden to these silent students.

Getting to Know Your Students

The process of getting to know your students individually, and trying to understand their interests, beliefs and values can begin the first day of class. Try to learn the names of your students as early in the semester as possible and find out by what name they prefer to be called. Also, ask about their interests and experiences early on in the course. On the first day of the course, in addition to asking students some factual questions about their experience with the subject matter, you might ask some questions that require them to give their personal feelings or views on a topic related to the course. For example, you could ask students in a literature class not only what books they have read in high school, but also what kind of a book or movie they would make if they had unlimited time and funds. This question allows students a wide latitude in divulging information about themselves, and it will help you see them as individuals rather than as members of particular groups.

Encourage students to learn each others' names and to get to know each other in group discussions. Use the students' names when you call on them or respond to their comments. Encourage students to respond to each others' questions and comments, not just your own. Some teachers have created an e-mail list for their courses so that students can communicate with each other and with the teacher in an informal way outside of class. E-mail accounts are free to all university members. Your departmental computer coordinator can assist you in using electronic communication tools to foster class discussion and sense of community.

Problem of Assumptions

No matter how objective we may try to be, many of us inevitably share some of the stereotypes which the media propagate about various groups. Such stereotypes are particularly evident for cases where the student's group affiliation is visually evident, such as racial background or physical disability. Although teachers should consider the potential needs of such students, it is equally important not to assume the student's needs. The well-meaning teacher often offends a student by offering extra assistance that the student has not requested.

The media and debates about Affirmative Action frequently have created the impression that African American students come to college unprepared and that they need extra help. A teacher, although well-intentioned, should never automatically assume that an African American student might need extra assistance. This attitude conveys to the student the impression that the teacher does not think the student has the ability or intelligence to do the required work. Teachers should always base their interaction with students on the student's performance. If the student exhibits the need for help, then the instructor can offer help. Above all, remember that students have different learning styles and that a student's apparent difficulty with the material may actually stem from a difficulty with how you are doing something in the classroom.

On the other hand, some students might have issues not evident at first glance that influence their learning. For example, a gay or lesbian student, or a student with strong religious convictions may feel alienated by classroom discussions or projects that make assumptions about their experiences or beliefs. In addition, a student's ethnicity is not always visible. These students' issues are "invisible," but may affect their learning just as strongly as the student whose diversity issues are visible. Try to anticipate issues of sexuality, religion, or other values for students as you give assignments and lead discussions. Look for warning signs of students who feel distress because some aspect or event in the course threatens their personal identity. Students may respond flippantly or sarcastically to an assignment, or voice criticism of comments made by you or other students. Or, they may become uncharacteristically quiet. In such cases, approach the student individually and ask the student to explain his or her objections and concerns.

Many students may not voice their concerns unless you actively solicit them. Give students this opportunity by using a mid-term course evaluation, about a third of the way through the course. A simple questionnaire will allow you to gauge how the class is working and hear about any concerns.

Assessing Individual Classroom

The students most likely to feel alienated in the university classroom are students from groups who hold less power in society and whose values are frequently maligned by "majority" society. However, students can feel alienation from the particular makeup of an individual class. In some cases, "majority" students may feel alienated because of the subject matter and/or student composition of the course. Caucasian and male students may find themselves in the minority for the first time in their lives in Women's Studies or African American Studies classes and may feel intimidated to participate in discussions. Some teachers have made the argument that it is positive for these normally privileged students to feel alienated so they can learn how it feels to be in the minority position.

However, if students feel they are under attack and that their opinions do not count because of minority or majority group affiliation, they may not be comfortable enough to open up to learning in the course. It is essential to make any students who are in the minority feel comfortable from the first few days of class. Ultimately, these are the students who can most benefit from the course concepts. Showing an interest in their learning and a respect for their contribution to the classroom will make them feel included in your course.

Guidelines for Classroom Discussion

The atmosphere you establish in your classroom is as important as your rapport with each individual student. You want to provide an environment where students will feel safe voicing their opinions and where they will understand that discussions are meant to foster learning. Students bring into the classroom a complex range of attitudes about free speech. Some students may make statements such as "I have a right to my opinion" while others may insist on the authority of special experience or knowledge, criticising other students by saying, "You don't have the right to say that, because you're not a woman/ black/Christian etc."

The instructor must find a way to mediate between the view that anyone can say anything and the view that only certain people have the right to speak about certain issues. While you do want to let students respond freely to each others' statements, you have a responsibility to restrict personal attacks. Many students who complain about the lack of attention to diversity in the classroom explain that they believe their teachers respect issues of diversity, but that they let students make injurious statements. Because you are the one who controls the classroom climate, you must be particularly attentive to the dynamics occurring during any given discussion.

Because issues of race, gender, religion, and class are so charged in our culture, many students bring to class considerable anxiety about speaking about these issues. You can reduce such anxiety by making your classroom a community where all members engage in trying to find out the truth about controversial issues. Diversity does not mean privileging "minority" points of view, but rather taking advantage of the diverse range of opinions and experiences so that all can benefit. Lynn Weber Cannon argues for informing students explicitly about the goal of shared learning in the classroom.

As one of her ground rules for class discussion, she asks that all students "acknowledge that one mechanism of institutionalised racism, classism, sexism, heterosexism, and the like is that we are all systematically misinformed about our own group and about members of other groups. This is true for members of privileged and oppressed groups." She furthermore asks students to: "Agree not to blame ourselves or others for the misinformation we have learned, but to accept responsibility for not repeating misinformation after we have learned otherwise."

By asking students to acknowledge that misinformation exists, and to accept responsibility for learning about that misinformation and not perpetuating it, you provide guidelines for group discussions. Most students do not simply want to voice their opinions. They want to leave the classroom feeling that they have learned from the discussion. Creating this atmosphere of a community engaged in seeking to uncover misinformation also helps you to move some of the focus away from the personal to the communal value on better information and critical thinking.

Setting Ground Rules

In many cases, teachers can prevent students from making hurtful statements by setting ground rules early in the course, especially in courses where controversial topics are likely to occur. In the first days of class distribute a list of ground rules for discussion that everyone should follow throughout the course. You might include general statements such those by Lynn Cannon as well as guidelines specific to your course content. Give students time to review the ground rules so that they can contribute to the agreement by clarifying rules or by adding others they feel are important. When problems arise during the semester, you or other students will be able to refer to the ground rules that all students have agreed on. By having students set ground rules early in the course, you have encouraged them to think about what constitutes a fruitful discussion where all students feel safe to participate.

These ground rules for discussion do not just prevent students from making injurious statements about others, but they also ensure fruitful discussion that focus on critical thinking. Even when discussing topics that are not controversial, following these guidelines, or those that you have established for your class, will help give students a sense that when they are talking, they are learning, and not just expressing their opinions. If you establish an electronic mail list for your course, you might wish to have students agree that your classroom discussion guidelines should also apply to any discussions that occur on the list.

Establishing a Safe Classroom

Establishing a safe classroom atmosphere is the key to increasing everyone's comfort level. As discussed previously you can begin by laying out ground rules for discussion of controversial, emotional and potentially offensive topics either in the syllabus or in a handout on the first day of class. Starting the class with a discussion of these explicit ground rules avoids some of the problems that may arise in the classroom.

Some teachers and students may find, however, that structuring discussion in this way inhibits the free flow of ideas. A handout on ground rules will help only if the course objectives and the individual teacher's personality and teaching style are compatible with such an explicit, "up-front" statement of rules. Some teachers address issues of diversity and the free exchange of ideas by introducing them as topics for discussion on the first day of classes, and by involving the students in the formulation of the ground rules. This approach requires careful lesson planning, but many teachers and students feel that it is worthwhile because it establishes a general atmosphere of open-mindedness and awareness.

As part of the opening discussion, the teacher might have students define and illustrate concepts such as "presupposition," "assumption," "prejudgment," "prejudice," "perspective," and "bias." Having introduced these words as part of the permanent classroom vocabulary, the teacher can now lead a discussion about the nature of opinions, how they are formed, and why they differ. At the end of the discussion, when the students realise what is at stake when they utter their opinions, the teacher can introduce the idea of the classroom as a place for the free exchange of ideas, where students should leave their prejudices and presuppositions at the door.

Giving the classroom a name such as "The Zone" highlights the important symbolic function of the room itself. Students may even build on the idea, making their own observations and jokes about the importance of protecting the atmosphere of this special place. The name, if incorporated into the classroom vocabulary, becomes a point of reference in all future discussions, and can be reinforced from time to time throughout the semester. With encouragement, students quickly learn to make observations about all assignments, readings and statements using the rhetorical terms they learned on the first day. Once sensitised in this manner, the students are ready to hold mature discussions about issues that might otherwise provoke hot emotions and name-calling.

Singling Out

A guiding principle for including students in the classroom should be to avoid the opposing habits of ignoring or singling out students. For example, in a discussion about African American women's experiences with poverty, a teacher might feel that she does not want to put the one African American woman in the class on the spot and thus avoids eye contact with her and does not call on her. On the other hand, the teacher might see this moment in class as a golden opportunity to make the student feel that her opinion counts.

By calling on the student in this context, however, the teacher has conveyed the assumption that this student will be able to represent the viewpoint of all African American women. In reality, this student may be aware that she disagrees with other African American friends on the issue discussed in class, and is reluctant speak for the whole group. She might also perceive the teacher's solicitation of her opinion as an assumption that she herself comes from a poor family. So how can a teacher avoid the extremes of ignoring versus singling out? If the student feels early on that she is treated as an individual in the class, that her opinion counts on all issues, she will be more likely to feel comfortable sharing her views when the class discussion of African American women arises. Particularly in small classes, where discussion takes place more often than in a lecture hall, teachers must develop strategies for encouraging all students to participate from the beginning of the semester. Above all, never ask a student to act as a spokesperson for his or her group.

Calling on Students

There are certainly advantages and disadvantages to the various techniques for involving students in classroom discussion. Allowing students to volunteer lets those who most want to talk have the opportunity to do so. It penalises, however, those students who have a contribution to make, but refrain from volunteering because they are shy, do not have confidence in their opinions, or do not feel it is appropriate for them to speak. In a 1992 survey on students' attitudes towards their education, almost 30% of students responding to the questionnaire reported having wanted to speak in class but not doing so because they "felt insecure, inadequate, or uncertain." The percentage of female students and African American students responding in this manner was somewhat higher than among other segments of the student population. Clearly, many students want to talk, but need encouragement from their teachers. On the other hand, calling on students ensures that all students make a contribution to the class, but can embarrass shy students and penalise students who really want to speak on a given topic.

Combining both methods leads to more participation in class discussion. You can combine volunteering and calling on students by beginning a discussion topic by asking for volunteers. When a student responds to your question, call on other students to support, add to, or modify that student's comments. Try to encourage all students to participate early in your course. The more time that goes by, the less likely shy or unconfident students will ever be to volunteer. Make clear in your attitude that you know all students have important contributions to make and that you have confidence in each student. Also make sure that you allow enough time for students to think after you ask a question. Many teachers only wait about one second for an answer. By waiting as much as five seconds, you allow more reserved students the chance to formulate their responses and to get up the courage to answer.

Monitoring Student Comments

It is vital that you, as the teacher, takes responsibility to ensure a comfortable environment for all students in the class. When students voice comments that attack or malign a particular group those comments potentially threaten some students in the classroom. In this situation, do not ignore such remarks, or change the subject. While it is unnecessary to reprimand the student directly, take issue with the statement made and remind the whole class that such statements are hurtful and do not further the pursuit of knowledge. Where relevant, challenge the statement's validity by pointing to statistics or studies that challenge stereotypes. For example, if a student makes a comment about African American women who take advantage of welfare, it would be instructive to point out that the majority of mothers on public assistance are, in fact, Caucasian.

To ensure friendly and constructive discussion, try to prevent students from attacking each other personally. Most often, the kinds of attacks students make on each other come from their perceptions of each others' background and experience. Students accuse each other of not having "the right" to speak on an issue because they do not have the experience needed to speak about the issue. Remind students that while personal experience can be a valuable resource for drawing conclusions, it remains only one resource which other personal experiences may contradict.

Anticipating Problems Before the Lesson

In addition to setting ground rules, try to anticipate specific issues that may arise during a particular lesson. Imagine comments that students might make that could be insensitive. Naturally, the more you have taught the course, the easier it will be to anticipate student comments.

Depersonalising Controversial Topics

When you introduce a controversial topic, you may make students feel less personally threatened by the discussion by introducing the debate in impersonal terms. Rather than asking a student, for example, "Do you think schools should make contraception available to students?" present the arguments usually made for and against contraception in the schools and ask students to critique or support the arguments. Students will thus be engaged in thinking about where they stand on the issue, but the more impersonal way of presenting the argument leaves the door open to students to decide how much of their personal views they want to divulge.

Teaching Resources

Anecdotes

Good teachers want to use examples with which students can identify. Good examples can make abstract and unfamiliar concepts more accessible to students. However, teachers who frequently use examples that reflect the experience of only some students risk alienating others. For example, the business school teacher who frequently employs sports metaphors risks not only failing to clarify the concept for students who are not familiar with sports, but also risks making those students feel that they are outside the "club" of students who speak this sports language. Another problem arises when teachers forget that they are already experts and use analogies that make sense to others in their field, but are foreign to the new student.

For example, explaining the causes of poverty in a Latin American country by using a classic textbook case study of poverty in an Asian country will not make sense to new students. Even if the study is the standard reference point for scholars in the field, new students will be unaware of such important discoveries and publications in the field.

Teachers should also remember that though they naturally draw on their own experiences when they teach, these experiences may differ significantly from those of the students. For example, comparisons with another country to which the teacher has traveled are often meaningless to the majority of students who have never left the country. Furthermore, analogies drawing on activities such as sailing or skiing, often associated with higher socio-economic classes, might make students from a lower-income background feel excluded.

Try to use analogies based on information you are fairly sure that students have. Use information already covered earlier in the course, for example. Also consider using examples from popular culture or from issues discussed currently on campus. If you do have an anecdote from your life that seems particularly suited to your material, make sure that you present it in a way that the students feel involved. For example, research on International TAs suggests that student interest and learning increases when the TA makes reference to the way things happen in their country. However, only when the TA "personalises" the discussion by comparing his or her life directly to the students' lives, does the comparison gain immediate meaning for the students.

Humor

Undoubtedly, the use of humor can open doors for students to take an interest in a course. However, humor is equally likely to alienate students who find the humor offensive. Humor can serve as a possible means of uniting people from diverse backgrounds, or a chance to lighten the mood of an otherwise heavy and serious class. But humor, far from being universal, is actually very rooted in individual identity.

Visual Aids

The use of materials other than written texts can make a course more interesting to students. Visual aids can be particularly helpful in the foreign language classroom. Be attentive, however, to the images you present to your class. Do the visual aids you use reinforce stereotypes of gender and race? For example, a Spanish teacher introducing the textbook unit on occupations may have students practice the new vocabulary by having them identify the occupations of people in magazine images. If all the images represent Caucasians, non-Caucasians may feel that they are excluded from this working world.

Likewise, pictures that reinforce gender stereotypes may offend men and women who believe such stereotyped roles are harmful. Of course, many magazines themselves perpetuate gender and race stereotypes, making it difficult for teachers to find non-stereotyped images to use in the classroom. Therefore, publications that serve women or ethnic groups may provide resources not to be found in mainstream publications. When drawing your own visual aids, try to present neutral figures of no identifiable gender or ethnic identity. Although it might require more time to adapt your visual aids to reflect diversity issues, it will make all students in the class feel included.

Role Plays

Role plays are often a good way to help students feel more

personally engaged with course concepts. They can, however, contain hidden assumptions about gender, race, or other issues. Whenever possible, design your role playing activity so that students play roles regardless of their gender, race, etc. Avoid assigning students roles based on their real-life identities. By arbitrarily distributing roles, you emphasise that the activity aims to teach concepts and critical thinking, not to reinforce differences between groups.

Group Work

The same principles of setting ground rules for full classroom discussion should also apply to group work. Students should engage in group activities confident that they will not be attacked personally or as a member of a group, and aware of the limits they must place on their own comments to other group members. When group activities are designed effectively, students can learn from each other and in an active way that helps them to understand and apply course concepts.

Assigning Groups

It is typical in classrooms for students to tend to sit next to students who resemble them. Thus, the seating patterns in a classroom will frequently be divided by gender or racial lines. These patterns of self-segregation are not necessarily harmful to learning, but they make it more difficult for students to gain new perspectives from their classmates. One way to encourage more diverse interaction is to assign your students to work in groups. If you let students choose their own groups, you run two risks. First, the students will choose to work with their friends or those who are likely to share their views. Second, students who are perceived as minorities may be marginalised when they are not invited to join groups. When assigning groups, mix different classroom areas, having students from the back work with students in the front, students from the left side working with students on the right side, etc.

Teachers have different philosophies about how to mix groups. Some prefer to have a strong student mixed with several weaker students, while others like to put samelevel students in a group. Remember that each scenario has advantages and disadvantages. You might choose to change your group assignments several times during the semester so that each student will have varied group experiences. In terms of diversity, you should try to assign students in a way that they will have the opportunity to exchange ideas with students who are different from them.

However, bear in mind that too obvious divisions may appear to students as singling them out. For example, if you have three African American students in your class whom you never assign to the same group, they may feel you are singling them out, or even penalising them for their race. Thus, if you change groups, make sure minority students work together sometimes and work separately at other times. The random nature of your choice of groups will make them feel that they are being treated as individuals.

Sharing the Load

Some students who are normally shy in front of the class participate much more when they have the opportunity to work in small groups. However, in some cases, the more reserved or shy students continue to remain silent in group work. Furthermore, students who dominate full class discussion are likely to dominate in their groups. Therefore, structure the group activity in a way that ensures that all members will participate equally. One way to do this is in your wording of the group activity. For example, in a group activity you could give the following instruction: "Every person in your group should give one example." In addition, during a follow-up discussion, always have a student in the group present the group's findings. Try to have each group work on a separate question or activity so that they are responsible for presenting information to the rest of the class. If you have a small class, have each student from the group present one aspect of the group's findings. If you have observed that a student in a group was not actively participating, you might have that student speak on the group's findings, thus holding the student responsible for the group work as a whole.

Encouraging Debate

Sometimes students have the impression that they must all reach the same conclusion in their group. By presenting the group activity as an exploration of diverging points of views, you send the message that you expect differences of opinion. For example, in discussing the characterisation of female characters in a short story, you could ask students to identify which characters the authors presented positively and which negatively. In a science class, you could debate the hypothetical outcome of an experiment before the class does the experiment or reads about the solution.

Ask students to make particular note of where they were in disagreement and to determine the source of their disagreement. Encouraging debate furthers the general goal of teaching critical thinking skills and can bear on diversity issues in particular. You can make the debate less threatening to students who are reluctant to criticise others' beliefs by using formats that are more like a game where students act out parts. Students in a literature class could put a character in a novel "on trial," while students in a sociology class could use the format of a popular television talk show to discuss attitudes about controversial topics. Such activities enable students to act out roles that represent different points of view. The acting allows them a safety cushion so that they do not feel personally attacked during the debate.

Syllabus and Class Assignments

The content of a course reflects a teacher's knowledge, interests, and beliefs. Identify your assumptions underlying your choice of topics and readings and the way you choose to organise your course. What seems to you like an obvious way to present the course content and concepts may seem either arbitrary or biased to students. For example, in a course on the history of political thought, is the history devoted to European and American models only? If so, why are there no examples from Africa or Asia? A bias is not necessarily negative. In fact, no one can teach a course without revealing their own experience with the subject matter. Furthermore, a teacher should feel comfortable about what he or she is teaching; the chosen approach reflects not only the teacher's knowledge, but his or her interests. The first step in getting students interested in the course is to share your own interests. However, you should recognise your assumptions and be able to justify the choices you have made in your course.

While you teach materials with which you are comfortable, you might also take advantage of opportunities to branch out. Examine the assumptions implicit in your course design. Are there gaps in your course you could fill by adjusting your syllabus? When possible, consult with colleagues who have taught the course or similar courses and compare your syllabus with theirs. Teachers often prefer to teach according to their own expertise and to avoid teaching topics in which they know they are not experts. But teaching the new and unfamiliar can help you to broaden your knowledge of the field, and also to rediscover some of the important course concepts from a different point of view. You might also explore tapping your students' special knowledge. For example, have students majoring in a related field give class presentations. By doing this, you will show students that they have knowledge to share with others and can actively shape the direction of the class.

Teaching of Conflicts

No matter what you choose to include in your curriculum, your choice reflects a particular ideological perspective. The great debates over the literary, sociological, psychological or artistic canon, and the controversies over "politically correct" agenda are unlikely to be resolved in the academic community as a whole. The battle between the "educational fundamentalists" who argue that it is possible to determine and to teach "universal" values, and the "relativists" who argue that values are never universal, but rather determined by specific cultural communities, has caused conflict within many academic departments. Rather than worrying about constructing the ideal value-free syllabus, which would be impossible to achieve, teach the conflicts about the curriculum in your field.

Let students debate some of the most interesting controversial points in the field. These controversies constitute, after all, a central aspect of what your discipline is about and can help to show students some key concepts important to the field. Pairing the sacred "classics" of the field with the "low" canon of popular culture can help students to ask questions about how certain literary works or scientific theories have come to be part of the canon.

"Lowbrow" traditions are as much a part of culture as the classics, and they may even determine what we will consider as "classic" in the future. Studying the relationship between "low" and "high" culture will illuminate the problems involved in deciding on a canon. Inviting students to join the discussion about a discipline's canon will make them feel more involved than those who are merely presented with list of accepted classics.

Teaching students that debate and controversy are natural and even desirable, and using debates among scholars in the field encourages debate between students. Graff also suggests that professors structure debate in their courses by bringing students from different courses together to engage in a "conference." For example, a modern French poetry class and the course on current popular film meet to discuss "Rimbaud and Rambo" and students are in charge of giving papers and moderating. It would, of course, be difficult to structure the work of other courses into your courses all the time. Take advantage of the controversies in your field to structure debate within your classroom and within your syllabus.

Tokenism vs. Integration

Because the student population is becoming increasingly diverse, try to reflect these diverse trends in your syllabus, particularly for humanities and social science courses where sociocultural issues are central. In particular, the results of the 1992 CTL survey at University of North Carolina (UNC) show that Asian students are more likely than other students to disagree with the statement "This course covered material from diverse perspectives, such as non-Western European views, women's perspectives, perspectives of non-whites, etc." Many teachers have begun to incorporate perspectives other than the male Eurocentric perspective into their courses.

Often, however, the intention to make a syllabus feel more inclusive can have the opposite effect by making "the woman's perspective" or "the non-European perspective" feel like an empty tribute to political correctness tacked onto the end of the syllabus. Where possible, try to integrate the diverse perspectives into other concepts you teach. For example, in a French literature course, rather than introducing your one African writer to exemplify the non-European perspective, contextualise this writer in terms of other issues you have already developed. For example, in studying the Martiniquan author Aimé Césaire, you could introduce him in the context of the surrealist movement rather than simply as the writer of African heritage. By doing this, you can still highlight the writer's non-European perspective, but you have shown that he is worth studying on his own merits, and not simply because of his ethnic identity.

In addition, avoid placing topics related to diversity last on your syllabus or last within a unit. This can give the impression that this topic is marginal to rather than an integral part of the course issues. For example, in a course on Impressionist painting, rather than leaving Mary Cassatt as the last painter because she is a woman, place her in a context in the course that has to do with her identity as a painter, not as a woman. Of course, finishing the course with a woman may be entirely appropriate for a conceptual reason. Aim to represent diversity while integrating it into important course concepts.

Assignments

The assignments you give indicate to students what you value most in the course. For this reason, choose assignments that both ask students to apply concepts and skills you have emphasised and that allow students to explore the connections between course content and their own interests and experiences. Avoid assignments that could exclude or pose a disadvantage to certain students because of their group identity or background. Not only could the assignment cause the students to perform less well than other students, but it also potentially sends the message that the field may be closed to him or her.

It might sometimes be difficult to choose an assignment that risks offending no student. In such cases, offer a choice of topics (of equal difficulty) so that students can choose the one with which they feel most comfortable. For example, in a French 2 class where students are learning vocabulary for marriage and family relationships, the teacher might decide to have students write a description of their ideal husband or wife.

This topic, however, asks students to reveal personal information they might not want to discuss with the teacher, and it could cause a particularly uncomfortable dilemma for gay or lesbian students. The assignment forces them either to lie about their ideal mate or to reveal private information. To make such students more comfortable, offer a less personal topic. You might instead ask them to describe the relationship of a celebrity couple, or a couple from their favorite television program.

Evaluation of Students

Keep in mind the students' varying academic strengths and weaknesses. For many students, performing under pressure, such as a timed in-class composition or exam, has a negative impact on their performance. Although you may feel the need to evaluate students in class, and may be required to give an in-class final, try to provide other formats that do not disadvantage students who have difficulty working under pressure. Offer take-home finals and papers, or provide options so that students can choose the format that will allow them to best show what they know. If you have students with physical or learning disabilities, they will often need more time or special facilities to complete assignments or tests.

Just as you do not want to penalise students who do not work well under pressure, be aware that you may penalise shy or reserved students by making participation a significant portion of their grade. Furthermore, when using participation as a grading criterion, make sure that students have the chance to participate in small groups, and tell them that their small group work is part of their participation grade. Make your participation criteria explicit to students. Keep them informed of their participation grade throughout the semester by giving them a summary of your criteria when you give them their first participation grade.

Grading of Students

Some teachers have structured their course requirements in a way that adapts to each individual student's needs. Students can choose early on how much they want the different aspects of the course requirements to count. The teacher sets a range of points within which students can choose. This system allows students to perform to their potential, but does not give them unlimited freedom.

No matter what kind of assignments you give, give students explicit information about how you will grade their work. This becomes a particularly important issue for students who may already be sensitive about their status at the university, or students who fear being penalised or privileged for their group affiliation. These students may have had past experiences where teachers singled them out for special treatment, whether the treatment was harder or easier than for other students. Your students may very well bring expectations based on these experiences to your classroom. Thus, when students see a set of grading criteria that appear objective, they will more likely feel a true sense of accomplishment when getting a good grade and understand the reasons when getting a lower grade. For paper assignments, give a list of criteria for A - F papers. If possible, give students an example of a good student paper or journal writing, and show them why it is good. Give explicit feedback on early assignments that will help students to improve on future assignments. When possible, allow students to rewrite for a better grade, since this kind of practice will help them to improve their writing.

Teacher-student Realtionship Outside the Classroom

According to a survey conducted by the Higher Education Research Institute in 1994 only 19.2% of freshmen said that they frequently had asked a teacher for advice after class in the past year. This statistic suggests that students do not initiate contact with a teacher outside of class, even if they do have a concern. Many university policies requires that all teaching staff hold regularly scheduled office hours in their departments, yet teachers often complain that they sit in their offices waiting for students to come. You can encourage students to come see you by scheduling informal consultations before the first assignment's due date. Even if the appointments are optional, by having a sign-up sheet, you send the message that you will be waiting for that individual student. Furthermore, if students have concerns later in the semester, they will be more likely to see you since they have already done this before in a neutral situation. Giving the class your e-mail address as well as the e-mail addresses of other students can provide an informal, non-threatening arena outside of class where students can pursue questions or concerns in a more relaxed manner.

Consider the time that you hold your office hours. If you hold office hours late in the afternoon or in the evening, when there are few people in the building, you may make students feel uncomfortable. Female students may be concerned for their personal safety if they have to walk to your building after dark, or if they have to enter a darkened building. When meeting with students, keep your door open or slightly open unless there is a third person in the room. By keeping the door open, you create a less personally threatening atmosphere in your office.

One way to make students more comfortable coming to your office is to offer both group and individual office hours. Students who typically avoid one-on-one office meetings with their professors might be more likely to come if they know that all the attention in the meeting will not be focused on them. For example, if you find that several students exhibit similar writing difficulties after the first paper, suggest to that they come to your office together, if possible, for a mini-tutorial in a workshop format. The students will realise that they are not alone in their difficulties and can learn from each others' mistakes. However, some students want and need one-onone attention. Do provide a variety of ways for students to meet with you.

If you are a younger teacher, students may take a personal interest in you, whether as a romantic infatuation or as an academic role model. Teachers should strive for an arm's length distance from students -close enough to be helpful and friendly, but far enough away that you don't feel any inappropriate obligations to them". Keep in mind that if you yourself are perceived as belonging to a minority group, some students from the same group may feel closer to you personally and seek frequent interactions with you outside of the classroom. They may even expect you to extend preferential treatment to them. While you should encourage such students to pursue you on a professional level, and act as a role model, you should discourage them from viewing you as a "buddy".

4

Testing and Assessment of Students

Teaching and other classroom activities are often seen as the enjoyable aspects of education, while evaluating student work and assigning grades are less appealing. Constructing tests is a serious concern of instructors and an important part of most courses. Tests given during the course of instruction can help instructors and students keep track of the kind and amount of learning that is taking place.

Tests given at the completion of instruction can provide important information about how much has been learned by the end of a unit, by mid-semester, or by the end of the term. Instructors can learn how effective they have been in facilitating learning for their students and, in turn, can use this information to revise their instructional practices.

There are two important occasions when diagnostic, or formative, testing is important:

1. At the beginning of a course, or before a given segment of a course, it is appropriate to assess what students already know about what is to be learned. A pretest can provide the instructor with information about students' strengths and weaknesses, and suggest ways to modify learning activities accordingly.

2. Frequent, short self-tests enable students to judge their performance while they are learning. Diagnostic tests can help students develop their skills if the tests are constructed in such a way that they force students to become more aware of the thinking processes they use. These tests can also provide the kind of rapid and frequent feedback that is so important to learning.

Different kinds of tests are appropriate in different settings. Performance testing is very important where the learning goals involve the acquisition of skills that can be demonstrated through action. In areas such as music, theater, art, dance, medicine, and physical education, much of the learning will be demonstrated through assessment of actual performance. The more common type of test in college settings, however, is the pencil and paper test.

Pencil and Paper Tests

Limited-Choice vs. Open-ended Questions

The term "limited-choice" is used here to describe test questions that require students to choose one or more given alternatives (multiple choice, true/false, matching), and "open-ended" is used to refer to questions that require students to formulate their own answers (sentence completion, short answer, essay). This usage avoids implying that one type of question is automatically "objective" and the other necessarily "subjective"-a faulty assumption.

The answer to whether it is better to use open-ended or limited-choice test items depends on the circumstances and on the goals of the test. Each type of test has its own sets of strengths and weaknesses. The advantages and disadvantages of the two main categories of test items are discussed below in terms of the various issues that are often considered when a test is being developed.

In principle, both limited-choice and open-ended items can be used to test a wide range of learning objectives. In practice, most people find it easier to construct limited-choice items to test recall and comprehension, while open-ended items are used to test higher-level learning objectives, but other possibilities exist. Limited-choice items that require students to do such things as classify statements as fact or opinion go beyond rote learning, and focused essay questions can easily stay at the recall level.

Since more limited-choice than open-ended items can be used in exams of the same length, it is possible to sample more broadly over a body of subject matter with limited-choice items.

A long-term goal of many learning tasks in higher education is the cultivation of students' reading and writing skills. Limited-choice items give virtually no practice in writing, while open-ended exams, particularly short-answer and essay, provide opportunities to improve writing. They do, however, favor students who read well, as these students have the skills to attend to keywords, recognise logical qualifications and cues, and discriminate among close choices.

Practice with writing is better provided by assigning frequent papers. Essay tests provide the opposites of what writing experts propose as preferred conditions for practicing writing. When scoring essays, writing quality should not be scored unless the objective is being assessed.

Limited-choice exams allow faster scoring than open-ended exams. Open-ended exams, however, usually reveal more information to the instructor about specific student strengths and weaknesses in processes such as comprehension and reasoning. Open-ended exams can also occasion more dialogue between the instructor and student.

Many limited-choice items can be answered in the amount of time it takes to answer one open-ended item, particularly if it requires a long and involved essay. Limited-choice items or the briefer type of open-ended items are more appropriate for quizzes and short exams than are essay questions. Unless graders are available, it is very difficult to give frequent open-ended exams and provide timely feedback in a high-enrollment course. Exams that consist mainly of limited-choice items are usually more practical under these circumstances.

Open-ended exams are much more difficult to grade reliably (consistently) than are limited-choice exams. However, to enhance reliability, you can use such methods as establishing model answers, working toward inter-rater agreement with multiple graders, and using holistic scoring. Being more limited in the number of questions you can ask is a weakness of essay questions. Requiring less time to answer few questions is a result of this limitation, not an advantage of this format. While it takes time to construct good open-ended items, it generally is much more time-consuming to construct limited-choice items because many more items are needed for the average exam, and because it is extremely difficult to write good items.

Experienced test constructors report producing as few as one to three "good" limited-choice items per hour. While it is easier to generate open-ended items, it is much more time-consuming to grade them than it is to grade limited-choice items. One exam consisting of only open-ended items may take as long to grade as an entire set of exams made up of limited-choice items. If the limited-choice exams are mechanically scored, the differences are even more extreme. In general, exams consisting of a large number of limited-choice items are easier to reuse than those consisting of only a few essay questions. This is because it is more difficult for students to remember and transmit a large number of questions to others who will take the exam after them. If a large item bank is built and different exams can be randomly generated from the same pool of questions, limited-choice items are highly reusable.

Limited-choice exams provide more opportunities for cheating than do open-ended exams since single letters or numbers are far easier to see or hear than extensive text. Cheating on limited-choice items can be minimised in several ways, such as using alternative test forms and controlling students' seating arrangements.

Multiple-choice Questions

Multiple-choice items are considered to be among the most versatile of all item types. They can be used to test students' ability to recall facts as well as their understanding and ability to apply learning. Multiple-choice items can also provide an excellent basis for post-test discussion, especially if the discussion addresses why the incorrect responses were wrong as well as why the correct responses were right. Unfortunately, good multiple-choice items are difficult and time-consuming to construct. They may also appear too discriminating to students, especially when the alternatives are well constructed, and open to misinterpretation by students who read more into questions than is there.

True/False Items Questions

True/false items are relatively easy to prepare since each item comes rather directly from the content. They offer the instructor the opportunity to write questions that cover more content than most other item types since students can respond to many questions in the time allowed. They are easy to score accurately and quickly. True/false items, however, may not give a true estimate of the students' knowledge since students have a 50/50 chance of guessing the correct answer. They are very poor for diagnosing students' strengths and weaknesses and are generally considered to be "tricky" by students. Since true/false questions tend to be either extremely easy or extremely difficult, they do not discriminate between students of varying ability as well as other types of questions.

Matching Items

Matching items are generally quite brief and are especially suitable for who, what, when, and where questions. They can, however, be used to have students discriminate among, and to apply concepts. They permit efficient use of space when there are a number of similar types of information to be tested. They are easy to score accurately and quickly. Among the drawbacks of matching items are that they are difficult to use to measure learning beyond recognition of basic factual knowledge, and they are usually poor for diagnosing student strengths and weaknesses. Matching items are appropriate in only a limited number of situations, and they are difficult to construct since parallel information is required.

Completion Items

Completion items are especially useful in assessing mastery of factual information when a specific word or phrase is important to know. They preclude the kind of guessing that is possible on limited-choice items since they require a definite response rather than simple recognition of the correct answer. Because only a short answer is required, their use on a test can enable a wide sampling of contentpletion items, however, tend to test only rote and repetitive responses, and they may encourage a fragmented study style since memorisation of bits and pieces of information can result in higher test scores. They are more difficult to score than forced-choice items, and scoring often must be done by the test writer since more than one answer may have to be considered correct.

Essay/Short-Answer Items

Short-answer items, those limited to fewer than five full sentences, are interchangeable with completion items. Essay items, on the other hand, allow expression of both breadth and depth of learning, and encourage originality, creativity, and divergent thinking. Written items offer students the opportunity to use their own judgment, writing styles, and vocabularies. They are less time-consuming to prepare than any other item type.

Unfortunately, tests consisting only of written items permit only a limited sampling of content learning due to the time required for students to respond. Essay items are not efficient for assessing knowledge of basic facts, and they provide students more opportunity for bluffing and rambling than do limited-choice items. They favor students who possess good writing skills and for their neatness, and they are pitfalls for students who tend to go off on tangents or misunderstand the main point of the question. The main disadvantage, however, is that essay items are difficult and time-consuming to score and are potentially subject to biased and unreliable scoring.

Performance Tests

The truest measure of whether a learner is able to do something is to watch the learner do it. Performance tests provide an opportunity to make this kind of measurement. As long as you are able to observe the student's performance of some prescribed task, your confidence in the student's ability is affirmed.

While we may see a performance successfully completed, we do not have assurance of the normalcy of the performance situations. We also do not know that failure to perform is an indication of what the student has done or will do in the future.

Different kinds of tests will be appropriate, depending upon some of the following general guidelines.

1. *It is important to base the test on the specific skills or competencies that the course is promoting.* A course in family therapy, for example, might include performance tests on various aspects that are covered in the course, such as recording client data, conducting an opening interview, and leading a therapy session. Developing a performance test involves isolating particular demonstrative skills that have been taught and establishing ways in which the level of skill can be assessed for each student. You might, for example, decide that the best way a student can demonstrate counseling skills, such as active listening, would be to have the student play the role of therapist in a simulated session.

2. *Good performance tests specify criteria on which successful performance will be judged.* For curriculum areas in which it is possible to define mastery clearly, it is desirable to do so. In most areas, however, effective

performance is a complex blend of art and skill, and particular components are very subtle and hard to isolate. In these cases, it is often useful to try to highlight some observable characteristics and to define what would constitute adequate performance.

3. *Define the task as clearly as possible rather than simply alerting students to the fact that their performance will be observed or rated.* It is helpful to give students precise instructions on how the test will be structured, including how long they will have to complete the task, the conditions under which they will perform the task, and other factors that will allow them to anticipate and prepare for the test. If possible, set up a new testing situation by asking a student or colleague to go through a trial run before using the test with students so that unanticipated problems can be detected and eliminated.

4. *It is important to give the same test or same kind of test to each student.* When possible, it is best to arrange uniform conditions surrounding a performance-testing situation. Students can be given the same materials to work with, or the same task. Often, however, particularly in professional practice situations, it is difficult to control the context of a performance-testing situation. One nursing student may be evaluated while dealing with an especially troublesome patient, while another will be working with a helpful patient. In these situations, documenting and allowing for the contextual influences on the performance is an extremely important part of the evaluation.

The effectiveness of performance testing is directly related to how appropriate the test is, given the course objectives; how clearly the tasks are defined; how well the criteria for successful performance have been identified and conveyed; and how uniform the testing is for all students involved.

General Tips for Effective Testing

- *Write possible test questions as you progress through the semester:* It is best to integrate test construction with other course planning activities. An essential part of each component of instruction is a method for evaluating student progress. In performance areas, instructors can plan tests that will ask students to demonstrate learning of a given procedure, technique, or skill. In areas where written tests are used, instructors can compose test items as they progress through the term, rather than all in one sitting. Doing so helps to avoid fatigue and will result in items that are presented closer to the way in which the information was discussed in class.
- *Use a variety of item types:* It is often advantageous to include a mix of item types (multiple choice, true/false, essay) on a written exam or to mix types of exams (a performance component with a written component). Weaknesses connected with one kind of item or component, or in students' test taking skills, will be minimised. If a mix of item types is used on one exam, items of the same type should be grouped together.
- *Be cautious about test banks:* Instructors should be cautious about using tests written by other people. Items developed by a previous instructor or by a textbook publisher can save a lot of time, but they should be checked for accuracy and appropriateness for the given course.

- *Test early:* It is helpful for instructors to test early in the semester and, if results are poor, consider discounting the first test. Students often need a practice test to understand the format each instructor uses and to anticipate the best way to prepare for and take particular tests.
- *Test frequently:* Frequent testing helps students to avoid getting behind, provides instructors with multiple sources of information to use in computing the final course grade (thus minimising the effect of "bad days"), and gives students regular feedback.
- *Test in proportion to the emphasis a topic was given in class:* It is important to test various topics in proportion to the emphasis they have been given in class. Students will expect this practice and will study with this expectation.
- *Show items to colleagues before printing the test:* Written exams should be proofread with care and, when possible, a second person should be asked to proofread them. Tiny mistakes, such as misnumbering the responses, can cause problems later. Also, check carefully for missing pages after collating.
- *Reuse effective test items:* If enough test items are developed and kept out of circulation between tests, it is possible to develop a test item bank from which items that are known to be effective can be reused on multiple versions or offerings of a test.
- *Do not use a series of questions in which answering successfully depends on knowing the correct answer to a previous item:* Generally, on either a written or performance test, it is wise to avoid having separate items or tasks depend upon answers or skills required

in previous items or tasks. A student's initial mistake will be perpetuated over the course of succeeding items or tasks, penalising the student repeatedly for one error.

- *Attempt to reduce students' test anxiety:* Instructors have found that using a little humor or placing less difficult items or tasks at the beginning of an exam can help students with test anxiety. The test performance of less-anxious students is a more accurate demonstration of their learning.
- *Pilot-test the exam:*A good way to detect test errors in advance is by pilot-testing the exam. Instructors can take the test themselves or ask colleagues and/or former students to critique it.
- *Be aware of the needs of special students:* It is important to anticipate special considerations that learning disabled students or non-native speakers may need. Instructors must decide whether or not these students will be allowed the use of dictionaries, extra time, separate testing sites, or other special conditions.
- *Bring extra copies of the test to class:* Having too few copies of a written exam can be a disaster. Instructors can avoid problems by bringing more copies of the exam than they think will be needed. Also, when duplicating the test, be certain that no pages are missing. Missing pages can pose a serious problem unless a contingency has been planned.
- *Do not interrupt students while they are taking the exam:* Before the exam, students can be informed that they should check the board periodically for instructions or corrections. Instructors can minimise interruptions during the exam by writing on the board any

instructions or corrections that need to be made after the exam has begun and then calling students' attention to them.

Helping Students Learn from Tests

Testing's most important function is to serve as an educational tool, not simply as a basis for grading. Not only do tests direct students' studying, but also they can provide important corrective feedback for the student. Returning test papers to students promptly is appreciated by students and conforms to traditional learning principles. However, if you do not plan to discuss the papers, do not hand them back at the beginning of the hour or you risk losing students' attention for the rest of the hour.

Although students appreciate your returning examinations to them, there may be some question as to whether you should return multiple-choice examinations. Multiple-choice items are difficult to construct, and you may not want the items to "get out." However, you can return separate answer sheets so that your marking and arithmetic can be checked. Allow the students to have copies of the examination while you go through the test. If you follow this method, however, certain questions arise. Does such a procedure destroy the validity of the items in future tests? Do the students profit from an exam review? These are experimental questions to which we have only partial answers, but evidence suggests that validity is not lost and that students do learn from their corrected papers, even when they don't get to keep them. Although you may not wish to spend class time quibbling over some individual items, you should make known your willingness to discuss the test individually with students who have further questions.

The comments written on essays and short-answer tests are far more important than the grade. What kinds of comments are helpful? Look for problems that arise from a lack of ability to see relationships, implications, or applications of material. Help students find alternative ways of looking at the problem rather than simply noting that something is wrong.

Comments that provide correction and guidance may not achieve their purpose if students become so discouraged that they give up. The motivational as well as the cognitive aspects of comments need to be considered. Misconceptions must be identified, but not in overwhelming number. Encouragement and guidance for improvement should set the overall tone.

A technique for helping students learn from mistakes while reducing their tendency to complain about the appropriateness or fairness of test items is a small group exercise. Instructors using this technique break the class into small groups of five to eight students for discussion of the test. Each group discusses the test for part of the class period. When they have finished, unresolved questions are referred to the instructor as the expert. This method seems to permit dissipation of the aggressions aroused and to limit arguments to points where there are several aggrieved students.

What about the student who comes to your office in great anger or with a desperate appeal for sympathy but with no educationally valid reason for changing the test grade? First, listen. Engaging in a debate will simply prolong the unpleasantness. If you decide not to change the grade once you have heard the student out, try to convert the discussion from one of stonewall resistance to problem solving. Try to help the student find alternative modes of study that will produce better results. Encourage the student to shift from blaming you or the test toward motivation to work more effectively.

After a test has been administered, a good way to judge its quality, particularly in the case of a limited-choice test, is to perform an item analysis. It is especially important to do this when test items will be reused or when there is sufficient doubt about students' test results to consider dropping some items as invalid when computing the final grade. Machine scannable test forms can be used or software purchased to provide item analysis. It is possible to perform an item analysis without a computer, especially if the test is short and the class size is small.

Prevention of Cheating

Coordinated efforts of faculty members and students is important to uphold academic integrity and combat academic dishonesty, including cheating and plagiarism.

The following strategies can help teachers to prevent cheating:

1. *Reduce the pressure:* The first action you can take is to reduce the pressure on students. While you cannot influence the general academic atmosphere that places heavy emphasis on grades, you can influence the pressure in your own course. One method to accomplish this is to provide students with several opportunities to demonstrate their achievement of course objectives rather than relying upon a single examination.
2. *Make reasonable demands:* A second way to reduce cheating is to make sensible demands. Write fair tests and design reasonable assignments. Some cheating is

simply the result of frustration and desperation arising from assignments that are too long to be completed adequately or tests that require the memorisation of trivial information. Remember, some students view cheating as a way of getting back at an unreasonable instructor.

3. *Treat students as individuals:* Work to develop and maintain each student's sense that she is an individual with a personal relationship both with you and her classmates. Students are not as likely to cheat in situations where they are known as individuals. They may be tempted to cheat in situations where they feel they are simply anonymous members of a crowd. If a large course has regular meetings in small discussion or laboratory sections, there is likely to be less cheating if the test is administered in these groups than if the test is administered en masse. Moreover, if it is in their regular classroom, they will perform better.

4. *Show an interest in your students:* Cheating is more likely to occur when students think the instructor is disinterested and unconcerned. Instructors often feel that any show of active proctoring will indicate that they do not trust the students. However, it is possible to convey a sense of alert helpfulness while walking between desks and watching for questions.

5. *Use alternate seating:* The most common form of cheating is copying from another student's paper. To minimise opportunities for copying, try to recruit proctors and administer exams in a room that is large enough to enable students to sit in alternate seats. Before students arrive, write on the chalkboard: "Please sit in alternate seats."

6. *Use alternate test forms:* Another way to reduce cheating is to use two or more alternative forms of the test. This method can be achieved by simply scrambling the order of the test items. Instructors who want the test items to follow the order that the material was covered in the course can scramble the items within topic areas.

7. *Be careful about extra copies:* Do not leave copies of tests lying around your office, the typist's office, or photocopy room.

Despite preventive measures, almost every instructor must at some time or other face the problem of what to do about a student who is cheating.

Alternative Methods of Assessment

There are assessment devices, other than tests, that can be used to provide measures of student performance, including:

1. Essays
2. Term papers
3. Research reviews
4. Reports
5. Case studies
6. Portfolios
7. Projects
8. Performances
9. Peer evaluation
10. Mastery
11. Simulations

Just as with tests, the underlying principles to keep in mind as you introduce alternative assessment tools are validity and reliability. A tool you use for measurement will be valid as long as it measures student learning of goals and objectives set for the course. The measurement will be reliable if you expect to get similar results administering the chosen assessment tool to the same group of people again. It will have the additional benefit of reusability, if it can be used in multiple instances, including future classes.

Available media and equipment influence the choice of assessment tools. But the principle factor involved in the choice of an assessment strategy is the overall design of the course. Good design principles demand that the assessment strategies be chosen as part of the overall instructional plan before the course actually starts.

Essays

Essays are written assignments in which the student is the source of information. Essays report on things the student knows or thinks. Reference is not a major part of an essay. But an essay requires the student to use high-level thinking skills. There may be preparatory activities involved with writing an essay. For instance, an assignment may ask a student to read several articles from several viewpoints and then derive his own viewpoint from the articles. The expectation in giving the assignment is that the student will apply reasoning skills and reach a conclusion that is well reasoned. The actual position reached is not the main value of the essay, and should not be evaluated unless your objective is to have students' opinions agree with your own.

Essays expose student-reasoning processes. An assignment of a practice essay near the beginning of a course gives the instructor an idea of whether the student's reasoning skills are adequate for pursuing the course. If a change in reasoning skills is a desired course outcome, an essay assigned near the end of the course is a good way to tell whether the desired skills have been attained.

Reports

Reports usually have a specific topic that may be assigned by the instructor or selected by the student. When a student reports on a set of facts or events, accuracy of the student's description is the main concern. The report often includes a provision for commentary by the student. The student's commentary is presumed to reflect the student's point of view accurately about the facts, events, or issues of the report.

Research Reviews

Research on which a report is based may be of any variety, including experimentation and documentation. The amount of research for a report varies. In a report based on documentation, credit for quotations and concepts should be included.

Research reviews ask a student to find out what research about a topic area has been done. Unless the student is asked to synthesise the results of the research, they offer little room for a student's free expression or creativity. If the same research review is assigned to a group of students or a class, duplication of the research found should anticipated. The assignment measures the ability of the student to use available research tools and the ability to judge whether articles found qualify as appropriate references for the subject at hand.

Case Studies

Case studies are often associated with problem-based learning. They are used to assess a learner's ability to analyse, make decisions, and solve problems. Case studies measure depth of learning to a greater extent than most limited choice tests, which focus on memorisation skills. Used as an assessment tool, the instructor usually creates the case that can be contained within the allocated assessment time. Like the case studies used for learning, these contain a number of circumstance descriptions, which provide guidance through the project. While there are self-consistent solutions, there are no "perfectly right" answers. Students look at the circumstances, bring them into their own personalised conceptual frameworks, and then try to provide solutions. Therefore, answers may be phrased in various ways, but must include all salient points and exclude inaccurate points.

Case studies assess the readiness of learners to use their skills in real world contexts. The student may expose both the process of working through a case and the results obtained. This allows the assessment to focus itself on either the process or the product. The student should be informed ahead of time as to whether process or product will receive the greater weight. Cases are equally easy to present in computer based, hard copy, or audio based form. They lend themselves to either collaborative efforts or individual efforts.

Student answers to case type problems may, with permission of the students involved, become models for answers to cases delivered in subsequent classes. If prior student work is used to model poor performance, care must be taken to keep the student's name and identity anonymous. It is probably better to construct poor examples if they are needed, rather than use student work.

The cases may require considerable effort for the teacher to create or select. The tendency to collaboration makes it difficult for teachers to assess individual contributions to team efforts. Case studies take a long time to grade, and grading of them tends to be highly subjective. This subjectivity is greatly reduced, however, by the use of guidelines and rubrics that specify what features will be assessed in a case study answer.

Case studies can be used with almost any available media choices. The cases can be presented in print, audio, video, computer based, or Internet-based forms depending on what the learners have available. Proposed solutions can be designed for presentation via any of these media choices. Where the Internet is available, the use of collaborative learning tools such as those included in Blackboard allows tracking of individual participation in collaborative activities provided all parties have agreed to use these tools. This means that where cases are assigned to groups, individual contributions to group effort can be assessed in a limited sense. A tracking system may note the number of contributions an individual makes to a discussion, but rarely evaluates the quality of those contributions. Checking samples from an archive of the discussion often gives a truer picture of individual student efforts.

Portfolios

Portfolios are of all the work that students collect as a demonstration of how their work has progressed and developed over time. The student, over the length of the course, will have been involved with and probably completed several projects. In most cases, it is wise for teachers to set standards for portfolio contents in terms of number, quality, and size of projects to be included. Fine and performing arts classes are likely to include portfolios among the assessment tools used. Other instances where tangible products result from student efforts are also good places to use portfolios. For instance, a business class may collect a portfolio that includes a business plan, some presentations, and an implementation timeline as evidence of completion of course objectives.

Assessment of portfolios encourages extended thinking and reasoning. Where privacy is an issue, the sharing of project contents may be strictly controlled. The student is completely responsible for decisions about what to include and is therefore led to considerations of quality in what will be submitted. Except for setting standards, teachers don't have much to do with the construction of the portfolio and are free to guide learners toward completion of their portfolio projects. There is a wide variety of media choices available for the types of projects that may be included.

Portfolios are useful in a wide range of subject areas. Besides the arts, where it makes sense to let students demonstrate their capability with produced work, such areas as writing and even mathematics have been assessed with portfolio type assessment tools. In writing, student style and organisational skills are demonstrated with portfolios. In mathematics, data analysis and problem solving may usually be addressed with portfolio work.

Grading is highly subjective. The teacher sees only the successes of the student and leaves all failed projects out of grading considerations. Grading of portfolios can take a long time. Portfolios can show development on a broad spectrum of work or allow students to concentrate extensively in very narrow areas of a field of study. This strength of the portfolio approach allows students to mask weaknesses in other areas. Extensive use of portfolios may encourage students to repeat earlier successes rather than to undertake new challenges.

Projects must be constructed in a media form compatible with the available media. Mediation of the projects in the portfolio to match the delivery system capabilities may distort the value of the project. For example, a portfolio of artwork loses scale information and impact when displayed on a 14-inch computer monitor. Where such distortions are likely to happen, the student should be made aware of them and requested to take measures to offset the distortions. Also, the act of handing in a portfolio puts at risk a large and potentially valuable body of the student's work.

Projects may serve as another basis of student performance assessment. A teacher may request one large project or several smaller projects during a student's course of study. The assessments of student performance on the project or projects collected may make up the whole or a part of a student's course performance. Monitoring of the student's ongoing progress toward completion of a project moves the emphasis of instruction and assessment away from outcome and toward process. Large projects create an opportunity for the teacher and the student to work with each other. Typically, a teacher will assign a large project to the student, then check the student's progress at various stages, offering advice for changes to be made along the way.

Students doing projects work outside the boundaries of the classroom. Classroom-time constraints play a limited role in how the projects turn out. Student effort is given to organisational activities along with problem solving. This allows the teacher to see the student's work at its pinnacle, much like a portfolio. Presentation of some or all of the projects by their creators can be a classroom enhancement activity. Students should know in advance whether all projects or a sample of projects will be presented. The student-to-teacher interactivity involved in most projects provides feedback to learners at the most appropriate time in a student's learning process-while a project is being done. Interaction between teacher and student helps keep the student on schedule toward project completion.

Since so much of the project is done outside the classroom setting, it is very difficult to monitor what the student is doing while completing the projects. Different levels of acceptable outside help may need to be defined. The pacing of projects comes from both the student and the teacher, and hence does not faithfully represent the student's own ability to set a pace. Getting the feedback to the student in a timely manner requires large amounts of teacher time, and frequent teacher check-ins.

Interactive projects are very well suited to Internet-based teaching tools. Tools for project interactivity over the Internet, such as "Common Space"are becoming readily available at low cost. The use of these complex tools greatly facilitates working with this strategy, although there is a need to learn how to use the tools that may take away from available contact time. Feedback on projects from the teacher must be timely, since pacing can be easily upset by long teacher delays. There should probably be a low class size limit to permit the teacher to provide timely feedback to all students.

Term papers

Term papers are valuable to students because they provide them with an opportunity to be experts in small but relevant areas of the field. They should be limited to one per term. Term papers are long for most students and are a significant part of the work for the term. A term paper should be introduced early in a course and collected near the course's end. It should contain some requirement for research, and a strong indication that the student has mastered the course material as it was presented over the term of the course. A term paper is a type of project, and the characteristics and recommendations for projects apply.

Performances

An assessment based on performance asks a student to perform. The performance may be in a classroom or at a special facility where performances of the type in question are done. Typically, there will be some measurement of the quality of the performance requested. The teacher alone, the teacher and the rest of the class, or a larger invited group, may view performances.

The criteria established help the student by clarifying what the standards of judgment of performance are, by letting students see strengths and weaknesses they have relative to these standards, and by establishing that the grading system used is consistent.

The number of available criteria that can be applied to measurement of student performance is incredibly high. No single checklist is likely to encompass every aspect of what students do when they are asked to perform. The richness of available criteria, however, doesn't make assessment of a live performance impossible. Instead, it makes precision in matching the choice of included criteria to learning objectives more critical than ever. For example, if you were making a performance checklist for a dance performance, you would almost certainly include some criteria related to the execution of the performance. But would you include criteria related to the choreography? You would probably only include this if the student was responsible for the choreography. Would you include a measure for the warmth of a student's smile while dancing? It depends on whether your instruction included any encouragement of the act of smiling as something that enhances stage presence.

You want to be fair to the students as much as possible in the checklist criteria you include. If your learning objectives are at particular levels, the performances on your checklist should be at the same levels. Making up scales and rubrics provides guidance as to how to measure what are often spontaneous and subjective performances. In general, students should be aware of the objective criteria on which performances are measured.

Peer Evaluations

The idea behind the use of peer evaluation as an assessment tool is that a student's peers, who have had to work with and contend with a student, have a good idea of that student's contribution level. The higher the grade levels of the students involved, the more likely this is to be the case. By asking students to review other students' products, results, or performance, the instructor gets to take account of experiences in which the instructor was not directly involved. Peer evaluation often involves the use of a measurement instrument distributed multiple times. This presumes that all of a student's peers participate in the evaluation. Sometimes, the number of instruments to be completed and counted may be reduced through varying both the assignment of partners and the assignment of which peers get to review. Some formula for compiling the instrument results yields an indication of each student's peer evaluation score. Peer evaluation, when used at all, should be only a part rather than the whole of a student's final grade.

Peer evaluation fills a gap in the usual assessment process that exists because so much of a student's performance is unseen. Peer evaluation instruments, while subjective on an individual basis, provide data through which a quantitative measure of subjective judgments is accumulated. The feedback of measured information to the student, in carefully chosen circumstances, may motivate improvements in student performance. Group dynamics are being measured with these instruments, which is important in environments that value active participation in collaborative activities.

Peer evaluation may measure student popularity or some phenomenon other than the one the instructor wants to assess. Although the instruments are used to gather data, the data is an accumulation of subjective judgments. Summary of the measurement-instrument results is time consuming. A set of standards should be provided and explained to students, or students may agree among themselves on the standards they will use in determining peer performance.

In computer-mediated, distance-education environments, collaboration is often a significant part of the learning experience. Peer evaluation is the only tool that measures this collaboration from the group's point of view. The negative influences of poor in-group performances by some students may be brought to light. Where computers are used to mediate the communications processes of the educational environment, they can be used to aid in the gathering and summing of peer evaluation data, thereby making peer evaluation strategies easier to use.

Mastery Models

When it is important that a skill be mastered, an "all or nothing" approach, similar to pass/fail, may be the best indicator. This is particularly true when a skill that will see later use in the learning process is first being learned. To assess using a mastery model, it is typical to assign a project that involves the use of the new skill, so that handing in a successfully completed project serves as an indication of the skill having been mastered. In many cases, the learner may take an unlimited number of tries without penalty, but will pass once mastery has been demonstrated. In essence, this model is like pass/fail for the steps along the way to achieving course objectives.

Mastery models are not competitive-everyone can and will master the skill. Such models have high validity and reliability, and they provide a clear and direct measure of success in reaching learning objectives. Students also have the ability to avoid the need to relearn redundant material.

Mastery models are only applicable in skill-learning situations. While they measure the mastery of a skill, there are different levels of mastery that are not measured beyond the minimum competency level. Because everyone passes eventually, mastery leaves open the question of how to give grades. When everyone succeeds, there needs to be a difference between A and D, but this method incorporates no distribution of grades that may be used for determining the difference. While applying the principles of mastery learning helps students get through courses, the non-competitive nature of the learning makes it difficult to assess inside a competitive framework.

Simulations

In an assessment that uses simulation, the student is placed into an environment that, in many significant ways, looks and behaves like the environment where learning will actually be applied. They are given opportunities to perform in the simulated environment. Some record of their performance is used as the basis for assessment.

The use of simulations reduces the student's exposure to situations that could have strong negative consequences if performance was done improperly in the real world environment. The classic case of simulated assessment is the simulated airplane cockpit that monitors student performance in handling the controls of an airplane, but will not crash. Simulations do not have to reach this level of complexity, however. Students have learned social skills such as job interviewing by playing their roles as if they were really going through an interview process.

The simulation provides a more accurate measure of performance than just asking a student to describe how they would do something. Simulations can be repeated to achieve continuous improvement until a standard level of performance is reached. The simulations have to be designed for each situation in which performance is being assessed. Designing and building the simulations is costly and time consuming. Once a student is made aware that the situation is a simulation, stresses associated with real world performance are significantly reduced, resulting in an inaccurate measure of the student's actual capacity to perform. The simulator must be tested and calibrated at the student's location. Many simulations are done with computers, and this makes their assessment results easy to pass on to other computers.

5

Teacher Training for Multicultural Classrooms

Multiculturalism can be defined as a philosophical position and movement that deems that the gender, ethnic, racial, and cultural diversity of a pluralistic society should be reflected in all of the institutionalised structures of educational institutions, including the staff, the norms, and values, the curriculum, and the student body. Multicultural education is the philosophical concept that all children should have an equal opportunity to learn in school, regardless of the children's race, social class, or gender. In other words, it is the recognition that of our common humanity and of the truth that our differences just make us different, not better or worse than one another. Along with being a philosophical concept, multicultural education is the reform movement and process through which this philosophical ideal can be achieved.

Multicultural education is a concept that is made up of four different components: content integration, prejudice reduction, equity pedagogy, and an empowering school culture and social structure. Each of these components must be addressed before multicultural education can be fully realised.

1) Content integration occurs when teachers use examples from a variety of cultures and groups to illustrate key concepts. When a variety of cultures are integrated into the classroom environment and subject matter, students have the opportunity to recognise, acknowledge, and address cultural biases and how these biases influence the way knowledge is constructed.

2) Prejudice reduction can occur through providing students lessons and other classroom activities that help them develop positive attitudes toward different racial, ethnic, and cultural groups.

3) An equity pedagogy can be established when teaching methods take into account the diverse learning styles of all students. When the pedagogy takes into account the learning styles of all students, all students have the opportunity for academic success.

4) Lastly, an empowering school culture is one that promotes gender, racial and social class equity. An empowering school culture holds the expectation, for both students and staff, that all individuals will be treated with respect and dignity.

Each of these above components must be addressed when modifying the school environment. For multicultural education to be implemented successfully the total school environment must be modified; just modifying one or two areas will not be sufficient. For example, textbooks that respect and recognise a wide range of cultures will not be effective in the hands of a teacher who does not respect children's different cultural backgrounds. All elements of the school environment must reflect multicultural ideology for the reform to be successful.

The broad goals of multicultural education are to enhance understanding, build relationships and self-concepts, improve multicultural climates of schools, and implement curricula that encourage multicultural awareness. Multicultural education allows students to see different points of view, gives minority students validation in the classroom, and decreases the amount of prejudice and misunderstanding that occurs between races.

Multicultural education not only educates children about the experiences and histories of students of color but it also encourages students to recognise the social injustices that racial and ethnic minorities face. Multicultural education empowers students to change the social inequalities that exist within society. Teachers do more than teach children basic reading, writing, and math skills. Teachers have the power to enhance or discourage a child's educational performance. They also have the responsibility to use children's cultures and experiences as vehicles for learning about academics, each other, and building respect for others. Teachers who value multiculturalism empower students to respect themselves, respect others, and become motivated to change social injustice.

Students bring to school, not only differing racial and ethnic heritages, but also a wide range of histories, perspectives, experiences, expectations, and approaches to learning. All of these factors will influence children's educational experience. The increasingly diverse student population requires that teachers have a broader range of skills and knowledge to meet these diverse needs of the student body. It is unacceptable for teachers to have little respect for their students, or to blame poor school performance on the fact that the student did not come prepared to adapt to the school environment.

Teachers must recognise the impact that cultural differences can have on children and children's education. Teachers who are aware of the impacts of cultural differences are more likely to bring children's different cultures into the classroom, which offers minority ethnic and racial heritage students the same opportunity for scholastic success as their white peers. Not only do teachers have the responsibility to integrate all children's cultural and ethnic heritages into the classroom to benefit the minority students; but, through seeing diversity as a cultural resource teachers can use the differing experiences and knowledge of all students to further each child's education and multicultural knowledge and acceptance.

Multicultural education is very important because it is the tool to change teacher thinking to maximise student learning. Multicultural education can alter preservice teachers' attitudes towards multiculturalism and the acceptance of diversity, which may encourage them to bring more multicultural experiences into the classroom.

The multicultural movement grew out of the civil rights movement during the 1960's. People of color demanded that schools reform so that the school curricula reflected their experience and history. The minority groups also demanded that the schools hire more teachers and administrators that were people of color so that minority children would have role models. In the 1960's and 1970's single group studies were implemented. Holidays, ethnic celebrations, and elective ethnic study courses were put into effect. These types of ethnic celebrations actually reinforce stereotypes and make minority cultures seem exotic or create the illusion that these groups only existed in the past. In addition, by celebrating different cultures separately from the Anglo curriculum, the view of the dominant group is maintained and the knowledge of the other racial and ethnic groups was selectively passed on to the students.

While single group studies actually amplified the differences between groups, the goal of multicultural education is to amplify the similarities between groups. Multicultural education is not a one-day celebration of a single ethnic group, but it permeates the entire curriculum year-round. Children given a multicultural education should have the ability to recognise similarities between groups of people, while recognising and respecting the differences between these same groups.

The multicultural education movement's goal is to modify and enhance the school environment so that all children have an equitable opportunity for academic success, to educate students about social inequities, and give them the skills to challenge these inequities. These goals of multiculturalism need to be achieved by the youth if they are to become successful adults in the increasingly diverse and global environment. Although the importance of multicultural education is recognised by individuals, it has received little legislative support.

Multiculturalism in the Educational Context

Multiculturalism realises the needs of all children in the classroom, not just the needs of students with ethnic and racial minority heritage. Although multiculturalism is concerned about creating opportunities for ethnic minority youth, it is also concerned with empowering all youth through cross-cultural interaction and teaching all children to respect differences between cultures. Multiculturalism versus cultural diversity. There is confusion in the literature and among individuals about the difference between multiculturalism and cultural diversity. It is important to note that these concepts are not synonymous. Essentially, the difference between cultural diversity and multiculturalism is people's attitudes towards diversity.

Multiculturalism not only respects differences between people, but also believes these differences are necessary for a healthy society. Cultural diversity, on the other hand, is the phenomenon of racially, culturally, and ethnically different people inhabiting the same geographic area. Cultural diversity occurs when differences between people are seen from a hierarchical perspective; one group of people is valued over another group of people based upon specific characteristics. When cultural diversity without multiculturalism occurs, the children who are viewed to be at the bottom of the hierarchy are especially at risk. But when this viewpoint permeates the school environment none of the children's needs are being met. When children are not taught to respect others' heritages, the educational system is not appropriately preparing them to function in the global environment.

The central goal of multicultural education is to provide equity and equality in education. Multicultural education looks at issues surrounding race, class, gender, sexuality, and disability and also recognises the issues that come out of these cultures. While some individuals believe that emphasising differences in the curriculum will inflame division, research offers the opposite conclusion. If the schools' curriculum silences students' experiences, differences, and criticism against the way things are, resistance will be intensified. Helping children know, understand, and accept differences can create a more unified environment within the school.

There are a variety of reasons why a multicultural educational environment is becoming increasingly important. The diversifying population and the emergence of a global society make it inevitable that children will interact and work with individuals from a variety of cultures. Multicultural education prepares youth to work with people from diverse backgrounds. It also encourages the development and application of critical thinking skills. When children develop critical thinking it allows them to understand issues from a variety of perspectives and also gives them the insight needed to define and address social problems. Because multiculturalism is very important, schools must align themselves with the characteristics identified as inherent in multicultural schools.

There are five characteristics that are inherent in schools with a multicultural environment. The characteristics include:

- content integration,
- knowledge
- construction,
- pedagogy,
- prejudice reduction, and an
- empowering school culture.

Content integration is the expansion of the curriculum to acknowledge the experiences of diverse groups, not just the experiences and point of view of the dominant culture. Through content integration, knowledge construction takes place. Knowledge construction occurs when teachers take the responsibility to help students understand how individuals' beliefs are based upon their cultural and ethnic heritage and life experiences. Teachers who strive to implement a multicultural environment also understand that the pedagogy used in the classroom must include strategies that lead to higher achievement for minority students. Traditional instructional strategies often include concepts or methods of instruction that are not familiar to students whose heritage is not of European decent.

Teachers who value multiculturalism also strive to reduce prejudice through helping students develop more positive attitudes about people of different races and ethnicities. Lastly, teachers need to strive to create an empowering school environment through examining the impact of school policies on students with different backgrounds and creating policies that help all students without hindering and unfairly discriminating against some students. Discriminating school policies can create a large amount of conflict within the schools. School policies that discriminate between groups essentially create two or more separate groups. If individuals are divided into groups they tend to favor the in-group and discriminate against the out-group, even if these groups have not previously experienced conflict. For example, teachers who create reading groups where each group is comprised of students of different ethnic heritages, even if ethnicity was not the basis for creation of the groups, may create discrimination between the two groups.

Thus, if one creates racial or ethnically homogenous groups through school policies that resegregate students, already existing tendencies toward stereotyping and discrimination will be magnified. Great care should be taken to avoid institutional policies that lead to resegregation and an effort should be made to adopt policies that encourage interaction between all children. A multicultural school environment assures all students are encouraged to respect the differences between people. Considering this country's history of racism it is important to understand the historical development and foundation of multicultural education.

While many states do mandate that teachers gain experience in understanding and working with minority groups, it is important for teacher education programs to take the initiative to implement these mandates. In order for multiculturalism to truly become a part of schools, teacher education programs must emphasise the importance of multiculturalism to preservice teachers. Teachers are seen as important agents of change and, as a result, effective teacher training programs and multicultural strategies are essential to this change process. Thus, various types of teacher training programs and strategies will be described in the following section.

Teacher Training Programs and Strategies

Although teachers' job duties are broadening and diversifying, teachers are often unprepared to meet the expectations of their new and expanded roles. Teachers are expected to be aware of diversity and to use multicultural teaching strategies and practices in the classroom. However, teachers cannot share and use information they do not know. According to Haberman and Post only eight percent of teachers are competent in multiculturalism. The types of teacher training strategies and programs used influence preservice teachers' abilities to appropriately bring multiculturalism into their future classrooms.

Preservice teachers are often educated about a variety of ethnic, cultural, and religious groups in a manner that makes these groups appear self-contained. Educating preservice teachers about different ethnic and cultural groups in isolation can lead teachers to believe that all children from a given ethnic minority group will behave in specific ways learned at home. Teaching about ethnic groups in isolation does not take into account how interactions with teachers and peers in school can influence children's thoughts and behaviors. In addition, by portraying different ethnic and cultural groups as self-contained, preservice teachers are not prepared to help children from different groups learn to interact and communicate with one another. Teachers must reflect upon their own assumptions about issues of racism and sexism before they are able to understand how students' differences affect perceptions of themselves. Preservice teachers who do not question their own race and class privileges or, perhaps have never had to "look at themselves" believe that issues of inequality cannot be overcome, and therefore are ill-prepared to deal with diversity and possible prejudice in their classroom.

In fact, a study by King found that many preservice teachers displayed dysconscious racism. Dysconscious racism is "the uncritical habit of mind, such as attitudes, assumptions, and beliefs, which justifies inequity and exploitation by accepting the existing order of things as given". Dysconscious racism may exist because of the struggle that preservice training programs face in defining multicultural education, changing preservice teachers' attitudes and beliefs, and developing competencies for a diverse classroom.

One method of combating dysconscious racism is to assist preservice teachers in examining their attitudes about whiteness. Whiteness, or white privilege, is a social construct that is supported and maintained by institutions and individuals. It is "a system and ideology of white dominance and superiority that marginalises and oppresses people of color, ensuring existing privileges for white people in the United States".

Many times white privilege is not recognised by Caucasian individuals in society. Many white people see white privilege as the normal way society functions. Often, preservice teachers express resistance to the concept of white privilege, or they believe that it is not oppressive to other groups of people, or they do not hold themselves responsible for the continuation and support of white privilege. An example of whiteness can be seen by the "pull yourself up by your boot straps" mentality that white individuals apply to everyone, regardless of preexisting societal or financial limitations of some. It is important to help Caucasian teachers to recognise themselves as racial beings and see how their lives and experiences have been influenced by their race. Preservice teachers must be educated about the existence and effects of white privilege. It is also important that they are educated about the effect of white privilege on those of other heritages.

There are a variety of methods teacher training programs may use to teach students about multiculturalism: the neutrality approach, the similarity approach, the diversity approach, or the "diversimilarity" approach. The neutrality approach ignores the issues and topics of race and ethnicity. This approach does not consider how culture and ethnicity influences various societal issues. This approach eliminates the controversy and discussion that may be involved in discussing race. By not considering the effect of race and ethnicity on individuals and society, this approach minimises the possibility of discussion and change within the classroom.

The similarity approach emphasises how various cultures are alike and minimises the discussion of cultural diversity and of racism. This approach allows the "melting pot" theory to dominate class discussions and explanations. On the other hand, the diversity approach emphasises how various cultures differ from one another. The emphasis on difference does not promote understanding between groups nor does it recognise the vast number of similarities there are between people. The "diversimilarity" approach stresses cultural differences and similarities. It recognises the similarities between people along with the social inequalities of the past and present, and contributions made by individuals and groups of all backgrounds.

Preservice teacher training must be transformed if teachers are going to have the skills and abilities to meet the needs of student populations. The first step is to recognise that a multicultural approach to education is not an addition to core classes; it is a necessary and integral part of the educational process that will lead to effective teachers. It must also be recognised that multicultural awareness is important not only for educators who plan to teach in schools comprised of minority students, but it is also just as important for teachers who plan to or will work in a school whose student population is comprised almost completely of Caucasian students. These students must also understand and appreciate cultural diversity, and teachers must be prepared to illustrate the importance of cultural awareness to students who may have not had the opportunity to witness cultural differences firsthand. Lastly, preservice education must also incorporate diverse cultural experiences with all kinds of students and schools.

All teachers must gain experience in working with diverse student bodies. Preservice teachers are often unable to incorporate multiculturalism into the classroom and often feel unprepared to teach children from a minority background. Cross-cultural experiences will allow teachers to develop an understanding of various cultural groups, along with helping teachers understand and create instructional strategies that take into consideration the diverse learning styles of all students.

Along with educating preservice teachers about learning styles of students, multicultural teacher education must also help preservice teachers recognise the inequalities that may exist in schools. Preservice teachers must have the ability to recognise when differences between individuals lead to differential treatment. They must also be instilled with the need to change these inequalities.

Multicultural education of preservice teachers must make them aware of how all of their behaviors either aid in social transitions or maintain the status quo. When teachers take social action against discrimination, they have the ability to change students' self-concepts and empower students to attempt to change their environment. On the other hand, teachers who maintain the status quo instill a sense of hopelessness in students. Teachers' multicultural attitudes have powerful effects on their students.

Current university policies often require multicultural education for those entering the field of education. However, many students enrolled in a multicultural course may be resistant to the concept of multiculturalism or training in this area. Resistance is seen in students who dismiss the course content, are silent, are absent from class, or who are hostile to the professor or other class members. At the center of resistance is the refusal to engage in discussion. Multicultural acceptance cannot be forced onto those who are resistant to learning and refuse to discuss their feelings and attitudes. How can teacher educators minimise the resistance to multiculturalism and make multiculturalism courses as effective as possible?

The relationship between professors and students influences the type and amount of resistance found in the classroom. The professor must establish a safe and trusting environment so students feel able to explore their attitudes and beliefs. One very important aspect of creating and maintaining a safe environment is having smaller class sizes. In this way students are able to get to know one another on a personal level. In addition, smaller class sizes help everyone get an opportunity to participate in class discussions and encourages quieter students to take part in these discussions.

While maintaining a safe environment, the professor must also push students beyond their comfort zones and help them realise that multiculturalism is more than just being nice to everyone and being open minded. If students believe multiculturalism is just being nice and open minded, they will not challenge their beliefs or attitudes. Teacher training programs must promote self-awareness and awareness of the influence of culture and racial heritage, sensitivity to the diversity of students, understanding of other cultures, and understanding communication across cultures.

Professors must also be knowledgeable about the topic of multiculturalism and tolerant of others' views and opinions. In a study conducted by Anderson, MacPhee, and Govan students who indicated that, they felt the multiculturalism course was a waste of time and those who indicated an increase in negative or stereotypic attitudes felt that the professors were not tolerant of their viewpoints and that professors were not adequately informed about multicultural issues.

Research shows that varieties of interactive teaching strategies are effective in raising multicultural awareness. Active participation in the class and in learning resulted in students with the greatest increase in self-awareness. A combination of strategies, such as lecture, guest speakers, class discussion, and experiential learning gives students a variety of methods and opportunities for learning. However, lectures only about specific cultural groups may actually increase stereotypes about these groups.

Multicultural classes should discuss current controversies in education and hear multiple points of view on these issues so that they can make an informed decision or opinion regarding these issues. It is also important to invite guest speakers so preservice educators can gain ideas and information from those who incorporate multicultural information and perspectives into their curriculum. Successful multicultural training also includes supervising cross-cultural field experiences and emersions into other cultures. Field experiences in combination with classroom training have had mixed research results. Some research, however, shows that a multiculturalism class in combination with a field experience leads to a positive attitude change and a greater willingness to seek employment in areas of high cultural diversity. However, if the actual field experience, issues brought to the fore through this field experience, and institutional racism are not addressed in a classroom environment, a field experience may lead to an increase in stereotypical thinking. If students' misconceptions and preconceptions are not addressed at the classroom level, the field experience will be interpreted based upon preconceptions and misconceptions and these will be strengthened .

Cultural emersions foster a greater understanding of what it is like to be a minority and also a greater understanding of other cultures. Emersion experiences increase preservice teachers' self-confidence and also lead to a change in attitudes regarding working with minority students. These experiences allow preservice teachers to learn from the community as well as their teaching experiences. The type and quality of preservice teachers' training influence how they bring multiculturalism into their classroom.

Approaches to Multicultural Teaching

There are several approaches to integrating ethnic and racial content into a school curriculum. The different approaches include:

— Contributions approach,

— Additive approach,

— Transformation approach, and

— Decision-making and social action approach.

The different approaches are occasionally used as steps when beginning to integrate a multicultural environment in a school. The school may begin by implementing the contributions approach and gradually modify the structure of the environment to move through the approaches, eventually reaching the decision-making and social action approach. One should be warned against implementing one of the three lower-level approaches without the intention of modifying the environment to eventually reach the higher order approach. The lower-level approaches have flaws, which may eventually lead to further discrimination toward groups.

The contributions approach is one of the most frequently used approaches. In this approach ethnic heroes and special days are inserted into the mainstream curriculum, while the central part of the curriculum remains unchanged. While this approach is the easiest to integrate into the curriculum, it does not allow students to obtain a global view of ethnic and cultural groups because different groups are viewed as just an addition to the regular curriculum. In addition, the contributions approach does not address issues such as victimisation, oppression, racism or poverty. Because of its failure to address issues of discrimination and inequality, the contributions approach trivialises different cultures and reinforces stereotypes and misconceptions.

The additive approach is implemented when various ethnic heritage themes and perspectives are added to the basic curriculum without changing the curriculum in a significant way. This approach shares the disadvantages of the contributions approach; it also fails to help students view society from diverse ethnic perspectives. In addition, the additive approach and contribution approach focus on adding information about many cultural groups to the curriculum.

These approaches either focus on the differences between groups so students are prepared to accept those who are different from themselves, or they teach students that even though people are different on the outside they are the same on the inside. Adding information about many cultures does not allow students to gain the critical thinking skills needed to challenge the inequalities and discrimination that exists in society.

Teachers who revise their curriculum by including literature and histories of women and peoples of color do not validate these people's voices; the basic assumptions and values of the dominant group remain unchallenged and unchanged despite the ethnic content. As one can see, multicultural education is more than a class, teaching style, or curriculum. Its goal is attitudinal change. Thus, it is something that must penetrate every aspect of the educational environment. True multicultural education teaches people to think critically and identify the various perspectives that form knowledge.

While the contribution and additive approaches recognise and teach about diverse groups of people, the transformation and decision-making and aocial action approaches teach individuals to critically think about how differences between groups have been socially constructed and interpreted. The transformation approach changes the basic assumptions of the curriculum and enables students to see concepts from several points of view. It also infuses perspectives and content from various groups, which help increase the students' understanding of society and different cultures.

The highest-level approach, decision-making and social action approach, includes all elements of the transformation approach but adds the requirement that students must make decisions and take action on issues related to the concepts that they have studied. The major goals of the decision-making and social action approach are to teach students thinking and decision making skills, which will empower them to think critically about white privilege, society, and racism and prepare them to initiate and support social change. The decision-making and social action approach not only teaches children to respect differences between people, but also prepares them to recognise inequality and discrimination in the school and work place and empowers them to take action against the discrimination.

Multicultural Pedagogy

Traditional, reductionistic pedagogy is currently the dominant pedagogy used in schools. In traditional pedagogy the role of the teacher is to dispense knowledge that has previously been constructed by others. Students are rewarded or punished based upon the quantity of information learned. The learning process, in traditional pedagogy, is not a process commonly used in any other part of a child's life. Traditional pedagogy organises lessons around a recitation script, in which teachers ask "known information questions," students answer these questions, and then are praised or punished by the teacher based upon their responses. Conversations between students and teachers are created through teachers quizzing students about the information they have learned.

Practices in place in the classrooms are usually not parallel to the communication practices used in family structures or any other institution. Thus, children's ways of learning and doing that have been taught to them at home often conflict with the ways of learning and doing that are practiced in the typical American classroom. Cultural mismatches in schools create significant barriers to student success because schools are created to serve a homogenous, Caucasian student population and not students from a wide variety of cultural and ethnic backgrounds. A multicultural approach to instruction requires that teachers learn how to assess and build on the personal, cultural and social strengths and skills that students bring to the classrooms, that they help students build on those strengths, and that they help students see connections between curricular content, their current realities, and their future possibilities. Teachers must become sensitive to and knowledgeable about different teaching and learning styles, the interaction between these, and how to fairly assess children who differ on these factors.

Multicultural instruction means teachers must understand that student diversity is a resource and it should be the foundation around which instruction should be organised. In order to best serve the student population, teachers need to create collaborative classroom environments, which allow students to become active participants in their own learning. Teachers no longer can assume the role of the dispenser of information, but need to act as coaches and resources that assist students in gathering their own knowledge. The new role of teachers and new student body creates the need for standards to measure the academic success of the school environment.

Multiculturalism and educational standards. Currently the use of educational standards is a topic of debate within the educational community. One example of a controversial topic is the use of high stakes testing. High stake testing can be defined as the use of students' standardised test scores to make decisions regarding grade promotion and graduation. Some believe high stakes testing is a good measure of students' learning and teachers' performance. Others believe that high stakes testing is biased against some students. How do strict standards fit into multicultural education? To effectively meet the needs of all students, standards and instruction must take into account the needs of all students.

Kluth and Straut developed a set of conditions to ensure that standards are appropriate and relevant for all children. According to these authors, standards should be developmentally appropriate and flexible. Standards must be created to measure students' growth from their current abilities to their future accomplishments not strictly to compare them to their peers. Standards should also be composed of many assessment tools and children's performance should not be based upon a single test; a greater and more comprehensive amount of information can be gathered using a variety of assessments. These assessments may include items such as students' portfolios, journals, classroom observations, and student-teacher interviews.

It is also important to ensure that all students, regardless of race, ethnicity, socioeconomic status, or disability, have access to challenging and stimulating educational material and that those standards are based upon this material. It is unfair to provide children with high needs or different needs material that is not interesting, relevant, or challenging to them. Lastly, the school community should work as a team when determining standards, how to measure the achievement of standards, and methods used to assist children in achieving standards. Having teachers, parents, and students involved in creating standards helps guarantee that they are fair and equitable. In addition, having students involved helps them remain motivated in meeting standards. Standards and the information obtained from them should not be considered only in relation to the student's performance.

The information gained from standards can be used to understand the current needs and weaknesses of the educational system so that strategies can be created to help meet these needs. One method to ensure that children's education and social needs is being met is through the creation of a multicultural classroom.

Creating a Multicultural Classroom

While the need for multicultural classrooms is high, there are actually relatively few of them in the United States. One must examine the reasons for the lack of truly multicultural classrooms to overcome the following barriers. First, the change from the well-known and dominating Eurocentric curriculum to a multicultural curriculum is slow. It takes time to educate teachers about the need for multiculturalism, the theory and practice of multiculturalism, and for it to be implemented in the classroom. Secondly, many educators do not believe that multicultural education is necessary in homogenous, Caucasian populations. Finally, many teachers do not understand what multicultural education is and how to implement it. Therefore, the lack of multicultural classrooms in the United States is primarily due to a lack of understanding and knowledge by those expected to implement it. Teachers must be educated regarding the importance of multiculturalism for them to properly implement its ideology in their classrooms. There are many considerations teachers must make in order to create a multicultural environment for children's learning.

- Teachers must evaluate their classrooms to ensure that their curriculum and practices are in line with multicultural ideology. It is important that teachers examine their curriculum for things such as stereotypes, racism, discrimination, and bias. One must consider each resource and every classroom material for what it is saying to the students. Often times children gain information from stereotypes contained within the curriculum or a lack of representation contained within the curriculum.
- Teachers must note these discrepancies and bring information into the classroom that will give students of all backgrounds representation, familiarity, and understanding of the course content.
- Teachers must also ensure that multicultural ideology is incorporated into every aspect of the curriculum. Multiculturalism is not a specific unit or class period

for its ideas and ideology can not be separated from the rest of the school day. For students to truly understand multiculturalism, its concepts and ideology must be present in every aspect of the classroom. In this way, students are presented with and encouraged to discuss past and current inequalities and unjust practices. It also prepares students to apply critical thinking and multicultural understanding to current and future debates.

Not only should the curriculum and the course content be commensurate with multicultural ideology, but so should the teacher's attitudes, beliefs, and actions. Teachers must present their students with an attitude of caring and openness so all students feel accepted and are able to learn to accept others. It is also necessary for teachers to realise that because of different opportunities and differing home environments children need different types of stimuli and environments in which to learn. Treating all children equally does not meet their individual needs, but treating them equitably does. Children do not need equal treatment; they need equitable opportunities to learn.

Cooperative Learning Groups

Cooperative learning groups are one technique, if implemented correctly, which will help meet the learning needs of all students. The method in which they are implemented also influences whether or not they will meet the goals and objectives of multicultural education. In fact, cooperative learning is used by both the traditional and multicultural pedagogies, but for different reasons. Depending on the reason cooperative learning is used, the strategy and the content, the practice may be very different.

Unfortunately, teachers are often taught methods of instruction with no theoretical reasoning attached. Teachers need to understand both theory and practices behind multicultural education for it to be successful in the classroom. Just implementing the strategies, without any reference to the theory will not change classroom dynamics nor will it empower students of all ethnic and cultural heritages to become active participants in their education.

Traditional, reductionistic educators use cooperative learning to teach cooperative behaviors. Traditional educational strategies place children into teams, and emphasise the completion of the task, require no interdependence between team members, and include no way to assess individual performance. Placing children into groups and telling them to cooperate does not ensure that they know how to cooperate with one another nor does it ensure that they will cooperate even if they know how. On the other hand, multicultural educators use cooperative learning groups because they are more compatible with cultures that value cooperation, and thus assist the learning process of students from these cultures. The goals of cooperative learning in a multicultural environment are to have children work together in small groups to achieve positive interdependence, and individual accountability.

Cooperative learning has five principles: positive interdependence, face-to-face promotive interaction, individual accountability, social skills, and group processing. Positive interdependence is achieved when students have to rely on one another to achieve the desired outcome. Within group processes can be put in place that will help cooperative learning groups achieve positive interdependence: Cooperative learning groups can be given a team goal which requires them to agree on strategies used to solve problems; assigning each student a role within the group requires that the team members rely on one another for task completion; requiring the individuals in the group to share resources requires cooperation among group members; and joint rewards encourages group members to help one another.

Face-to-face promotive interaction among students exists when they help and support each other's learning and success. Individual accountability is created when results of each individual's performance are given to the individual and the team; by giving the team the results of an individual's performance the team can better assess who needs help with the materials and assignments. Social skills are essential for cooperative learning. Social skills are used more often when teams are given bonus points each time a member uses specific social skills. Peer evaluations also help students recognise their place within the group and what social skills they need to work on. Lastly, group processing is used to determine if the goals were met, to look at the relationships among group members, and to evaluate the efficacy of the team's functioning. In order for cooperative learning groups, or any multicultural instructional strategy, to be implemented correctly teachers must be trained in the theory, necessity, and practices of multicultural education. Teachers must be trained so they have the ability to individualise learning programs to attempt to meet all children's needs.

Effects of Teachers' Multicultural Awareness

Teachers view multiculturalism in a variety of different ways. In a study conducted by Banister and Maher four themes were identified around teachers' conceptions of multicultural education:

1) Multiculturalism means diversity;

2) Multiculturalism is accepting difference and encouraging assimilation

3) We don't need "it" here, and

4) We lack the resources and the means.

Multiculturalism means diversity was presented through teachers' descriptions of their student populations as culturally diverse and therefore multicultural. When teachers understand multiculturalism as classroom diversity it is reduced to superficial elements and does not increase students awareness of one another or society.

The attitudes that multiculturalism is difference and the melting pot occured when teachers spoke of their desire to value differences in conjunction with their description of how distinctions fade as cultures become integrated. This melting pot theory has maintained Western values in schools not allowing integration of ideas from other cultures. For these teachers, respect for other cultures meant learning about them with an underlying assumption that they eventually melt into the dominant culture.

Teachers who said they did not need multiculturalism at their school because their student population was homogenous expressed the we don't need "it" here view. This attitude increases Caucasian students' Eurocentric view by creating an in-group/out-group attitude and atmosphere within the school. Teachers who claimed that they lacked the resources and the means stated that they did not have time, materials, or support from administrators. It is important that teachers receive support for implementing multicultural curriculum through release time, wider availability of resources, and administrative support. By viewing multiculturalism as something that must take up space in the curriculum at the expense of more important agendas, teachers can dismiss the possibilities of the multicultural perspective.

The understanding of multiculturalism and use of multicultural curricula also have direct effect on youths' academic success. When students' different cultures, tools, language, and symbols are used in the classroom, learning is made easier and the students become competent at functioning in more than one culture. When the learning styles and needs of children are considered, they are more likely to be successful in the educational environment.

Recognition, acceptance, and sensitivity to cultural and ethnic factors lead to schools with lower rates of dropouts and problem behaviors. Hillard asserted that the largest source of variation in school achievement among students is variation in the quality of teaching services. Many students of color view teachers as greater threats of racist attitudes than fellow students, because teachers have the authority and power to overrule them. In addition, when teachers allow racist attitudes to permeate the school, the safety of minority students is threatened.

A critical step in providing multicultural education involves the cultural awareness and sensitivity of teachers. Teachers interact with students on a daily basis, so their perceptions of multiculturalism are very important. A teacher's beliefs may influence that teacher's actions in ways he or she may not be aware of. A teacher's beliefs can be shown by whom the teacher calls on and whom he does not, and who is praised and for what. In addition, teachers' unconscious nonverbal signals can significantly influence a child's self-concept and self-expectations. Teachers' daily contact and interaction with students may have a long-term impact on students' beliefs and attitudes. Students internalise the subtle messages portrayed in the teachers' actions and statements.

Gilbert and Gay found that teachers' attitudes and perceptions of students influence teachers' expectations and treatment of these students. Race, along with sex and social class, are factors that can influence teachers' conscious and unconscious expectations of students. Studies by Gay have found that both Mexican American students and African American students were not given as many opportunities to participate in classroom interactions with teachers. These students had fewer and easier questions asked of them, had less time to give a response to the questions, and were given less praise for a response than the Euro-American students.

A study by Roscigno and Ainsworth-Darnell found that teachers' perceptions of students' academic track, attentiveness in class, completion of homework, and effort put into schoolwork was significantly lower for African American students than for white students. Research shows that teachers have lower expectations for ethnic minority youth. Teachers' low expectations get played out in interpersonal interactions, but also in instructional programs, such as allowing access to gifted programs to students who are already performing well academically and giving the watered down curriculum to students who are not performing well academically.

Teachers' expectations can become a self-fulfilling prophecy for the student even when there is no real evidence for the teachers' expectations. This can be seen through the increasingly poorer performance of minority children the longer that they stay in school. In the early grades the achievement of minority students is similar to the achievement of white students. The longer the minority students stay within the school system, the more their achievement lags behind the achievement of white students. Another way that the teacher's beliefs about the abilities of the students can influence the students' academic achievement is through the "Pygmalion effect." The Pygmalion effect describes the fact that people achieve at the level at which they are expected to achieve. If a teacher believes that children of color can only perform at a remedial level, these children will perform at this level because this is what is expected of them.

Teachers are in an influential position with respect to students and can communicate significant messages concerning expectations, evaluations, and performance. Children's social learning is influenced by modeling. Teachers' multicultural attitudes can influence children's' school performances through teachers' modeling of correct or incorrect behaviors or through teachers' expectations of the abilities and achievements of the minority students. While teachers' multicultural attitudes can be influential on students' academic success; the influence of the overall school environment is also critical to students' academic and social success.

Creating a Multicultural School Environment

Because the school is the major institution of socialisation, it is a critical arena in which inequality is perpetuated. Until recently the school has acted as the melting pot, indoctrinating children to the white middle-class culture. However, schools have the ability to spread the ideology of multiculturalism and create an environment and student body that values acceptance or it can create an environment that breeds racism and discrimination. Children are aware of racial differences before entering school, but the school can influence a child's attitudes towards these differences.

Children come to school with preconceived ideas regarding the issue of diversity. In fact, six-month-old infants notice skin color differences and two-year-old children began to ask questions regarding skin color differences. Awareness of racial and ethnic differences develops until the age of nine years. After nine years of age, children's views on diversity tend to remain constant unless altered by life-changing events. Therefore, it is important for schools to address racial differences early and effectively in the school curriculum, so children can be exposed to positive attitudes towards racial differences.

A study performed by Wham, Barnhart, and Cook found that without a diversity program children's appreciation of diversity might even decline over the course of a given school year.

Shirley investigated the effects of integrating multicultural activities into English, social studies, and reading curricula on the self-concept, racial attitudes, and achievement of students in racially integrated fifth-and sixth-grade classes. There were no statistically significant changes in the self-concept and achievement levels of African-American students in the experimental groups. However, the racial attitudes of the white students in the experimental groups became more positive than the racial attitudes of the white students in the control groups. It is not only important, but also necessary, to evaluate teachers and students' levels of multicultural awareness. Only through the proper implementation of multiculturalism can all students receive the education that is necessary for their success. Many preservice teachers who value multiculturalism may be placed into environments where the ideology of multiculturalism is not in practice. Teachers must be knowledgeable about methods and strategies that can be used to increase the level of multiculturalism within school environments.

In schools, many plans for establishing multiculturalism use the teachers as vehicles of knowledge. Pullen suggests that a series of in-service workshops will assist in preparing teachers in creating multicultural school environments. The workshops consist of four phases: self-inventory, mini-lectures, a multicultural mentoring program, and a mandatory multicultural lesson. The self-inventory portion provides teacher a measure of their cultural awareness and tolerance. Mini-lectures are presented by individuals of a wide-range of ethnicities, which may include students, teachers, and professors of multicultural education.

A multicultural mentoring program will allow teachers of different ethnicities to share in question and answer sessions that may help lead to understanding and education. After teachers have completed the first three phases of the workshops, they are required to teach a multicultural lesson based upon the information that they received at the workshops.

For teachers to be effective in implementing a multicultural program in their classrooms and schools, they must have the ability to recognise their feelings and attitudes as part of their cultural norms and biases. Teachers must also recognise the value of ethnic and cultural diversity as a basis for societal enrichment, cohesiveness, and survival. They must also know in detail about experiences, viewpoints, and needs of various cultural groups so that they are able to teach their students about these different groups. Teachers need to acquire sensitivity to words and actions insulting or hurtful to minority groups so they can be aware of their own biases and discrimination towards different groups, and also discourage students' actions and words that may be hurtful to individuals. Teachers must use various classroom techniques to demonstrate how people of various cultures and backgrounds can communicate effectively and work cooperatively. Lastly, teachers must evaluate instructional materials to make sure that they are unbiased and factual and complete in describing the influence and contributions of individuals of minority race.

According to Gallagher, the pre-packaged multicultural school environment plans are easy to implement, but often do not address all of the needs of a particular school and community environment. As in any change effort, the active involvement of the school community is necessary. Bernard advocates community involvement, which includes the establishment of a multicultural task force consisting of youth, teachers, parents, principal, school personnel, and community representatives from a wide variety of cultures and backgrounds. The task force must create a mission statement/policy that embraces the philosophy that the school is committed to all students receiving an education that affirms human diversity and validates the history and culture of all ethnic groups, based on high expectations for academic success for all students, and encourages students' active participation in the school.

The school environment must be modified so that the community can be formed through communication and establishing bonds between individuals. It is important that the students take the opportunity to be open and honest with one another and learn from one another. Differences and similarities must be challenged and examined to create a stronger community. Bernard ascertains that when modifying the structure of the school environment, it is important to redistribute power and authority in the classroom in a manner that empowers ethnic minority children and allows all teachers and youth to work together. Redistribution of power in this manner leads to equality in the schools. In addition, teachers must hold high expectations for ethnic minority children because a teacher's expectations about a student have a very powerful effect on the student. In fact, teachers' expectations can influence a student even when students' hold negative attitudes towards the teacher. Lastly, multicultural content must be infused throughout the curriculum. This can be accomplished by placing value the primary language of minority children, not stereotyping learning styles of ethnic minority children, and hiring ethnic minority teachers, teachers with a second-language competency, and teachers with English as Second Language training.

6

Teachers in Online Learning Environment

Learning and teaching in an online environment are, in many ways, much like teaching and learning in any other formal educational context: learners' needs are assessed; content is negotiated or prescribed; learning activities are orchestrated; and learning is assessed. However, the pervasive effect of the online medium creates a unique environment for teaching and learning. The most compelling feature of this context is the capacity for shifting the time and place of the educational interaction. Next comes the ability to support content encapsulated in many formats, including multimedia, video, and text, which gives access to learning content that exploits all media attributes. Third, the capacity of the Net to access huge repositories of content on every conceivable subject—including content created by the teacher and fellow students—creates learning and study resources previously available only in the largest research libraries, but now accessible in every home and workplace. Finally, the capacity to support human and machine interaction in a variety of formats in both asynchronous and synchronous modalities creates a communications-rich learning context.

To provide a mental schema for thinking about learning and teaching in this context, Garrison, Anderson, and Archer developed a conceptual model of online learning that they referred to as a "community of learning" model. This model (Figure 1) postulates that deep and meaningful learning results when there are sufficient levels of three component "presences."

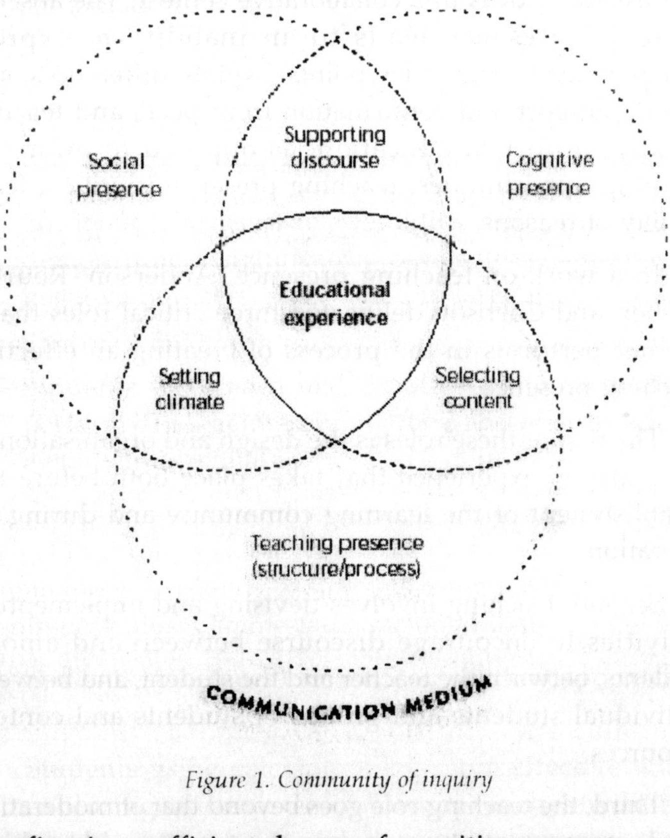

Figure 1. Community of inquiry

The first is a sufficient degree of cognitive presence, such that serious learning can take place in an environment that supports the development and growth of critical thinking skills. Cognitive presence is grounded in and defined by study of a particular content; thus, it works within the epistemological, cultural, and social expression of the content in an approach that supports the development of critical thinking skills.

The second, social presence, relates to the establishment of a supportive environment such that students feel the necessary degree of comfort and safety to express their ideas in a collaborative context. The absence of social presence leads to an inability to express disagreements, share viewpoints, explore differences, and accept support and confirmation from peers and teacher. Finally, in formal education, as opposed to infor-mal learning opportunities, teaching presence is critical for a variety of reasons.

In a work on teaching presence, Anderson, Rourke, Archer, and Garrison delineated three critical roles that a teacher performs in the process of creating an effective teaching presence.

The first of these roles is the design and organisation of the learning experience that takes place both before the establishment of the learning community and during its operation.

Second, teaching involves devising and implementing activities to encourage discourse between and among students, between the teacher and the student, and between individual students and groups of students and content resources.

Third, the teaching role goes beyond that of moderating the learning experiences when the teacher adds subject matter expertise through a variety of forms of direct instruction.

The creation of teaching presence is not always the sole task of the formal teacher. In many contexts, especially when teaching at senior university level, teaching presence is delegated to or assumed by students as they contribute their own skills and knowledge to the developing learning community. In addition to these tasks, in formal education, the institution and its teacher employees are usually fulfilling a critical credentialing role that involves the assessment and certification of student learning.

DESIGNING OF ONLINE LEARNING ENVIRONMENT

The design and construction of the course content, learning activities, and assessment framework constitute the first opportunity for teachers to develop their "teacher presence." The role the teacher plays in creating and maintaining the course contents varies from that of a tutor working with materials and an instructional design created by others, to that of "lone ranger," in which the teacher creates all of the content.

Regardless of the formal role of the teacher, online learning creates an opportunity for flexibility and revision of content in situ that was not provided by older forms of mediated teaching and learning. The vast educational and content resources of the Net, and its capacity to support many different forms of interaction, allow for negotiation of content and activity, and a corresponding increase in autonomy and control. Teachers are no longer confined to the construction of monolithic packages that are not easily modified in response to student need. Rather, the design and organisation of activities within the learning community can proceed while the course is in progress.

Such flexibility is not without cost, as customisation of any product is more expensive than mass production of a standardised product. Thus, the effective online learning teacher makes provision for negotiation of activities, or even content, to satisfy unique learning needs. However, within this flexibility, the need to stimulate, guide, and support learning remains. These tasks include the design of a series of learning activities that encourage independent study and community building, that deeply explore content knowledge, that provide frequent and diverse forms of formative assessment, and that respond to common and unique student needs and aspirations.

The design of e-learning courses provides opportunities for teachers to instil their own teaching presence by establishing a personalised tone within the course content. This is done by allowing students to see the personal excitement and appeal that inspires the teacher's interest in the subject. Borge Holmberg first wrote about a style of expression, referred to as "guided didactic interaction," that presents content in a conversational style. This writing style helps the learner identify, in a personalised way, with the teacher.

Techniques such as illustration of content issues with personal reflections, anecdotes, and discussions of the teacher's own struggles and successes as they have gained mastery of the content have been found to be inspirational and motivating to students. Activities in this category of teaching presence include building curriculum materials. The cost of creating high quality, interactive learning resources has led to renewed interest in reusing content encapsulated and formally described through metadata as "learning objects". These objects are then made accessible in repositories such as Multimedia Educational Resource for Learning and Online Teaching or the Campus Alberta Repository of Educational Objects.

Creating or repurposing materials, such as lecture notes, to provide online teacher commentaries, mini-lectures, personal insights, and other customised views of course content, is another common activity that we assign to the category of teaching presence. We anticipate that work on educational standards for describing, storing, and sequencing of educational content, and for formally modeling the way in which learning activities are designed, will significantly change the design role of many teachers from one of content creation, to one of customisation, application and contextualisation of learning sequences.

This design category of teaching presence also includes the processes through which the instructor negotiates time lines for group activities and student project work, a critical coordinating and motivating function of formal online course design and development, and a primary means of setting and maintaining teaching presence.

The modern Web supports a number of media, each of which can be incorporated into the design of an online learning course. However, getting the mix right between opportunities for synchronous and asynchronous interaction, and group and independent study activities remains a challenge.

There are two competing models of online learning, each of which has strong adherents and a growing body of research and theoretical rationales for its effective application. The first, the community of learning model, uses real-time synchronous or asynchronous communication technologies to create virtual classrooms that are often modeled, both pedagogically and structurally, on the campus classroom. This model evolved from telephone-based audio conferencing. Its evolution to the Net has allowed for delivery directly to the learner's office and home, thereby bypassing expensive remote learning centres that were a feature of older virtual classroom models.

More recently, popular Web-based computer conferencing systems allow for asynchronous collaboration among and between student and teachers. The synchronous virtual classroom model has advantages, in that it is a familiar educational model with a great deal of similarity to teaching and learning in campus-based classrooms. It provides increased access by spanning geographic distance; however, it constrains participants in terms of a single time that they must be present. This problem is compounded when a class spans many time zones.

The asynchronous version of the virtual classroom overcomes the temporal limitations, but can result in a shortage of coordination and reduce opportunities for students to feel "in sync" with the class. Designing effective online courses will increasingly involve judicious selection of combinations of media and format that balance the differential capacities of media to support the creation of social and cognitive presence, with the educational need for variety, the special communications characteristics demanded of particular content, and the cost, access, and training requirements of the media.

The second model of online learning involves independent learners who work by themselves and at their own pace through the course of instruction. This model maximises flexibility, but it challenges the institution's capacity to facilitate group social or collaborative learning activities. The "independent study model" is almost always selected in online learning models that allow for continuous enrolment or "just-in-time" access to educational content. It is very challenging to create collaborative learning or social activities when students are at very different places in the curriculum. Fortunately, it is possible to combine synchronous, asynchronous, and independent study activities in a single course.

Many institutions are developing both paced and unpaced models of delivery to accommodate student learning preferences and needs. Within a single class, it is possible to offer optional synchronous activities, and teachers usually build a real time Net-based audio graphic session into the beginning section of classes. This session allows them to get to know the students from both a personal and professional viewpoint, explore their aspirations for the course, discuss assessment activities, and provide an opportunity for students to ask any pressing questions. Synchronous activities are also useful for guest interviews, for special activities such as debates and presentations, and of course, for holding the end of class social gathering-parties held in asynchronous time never seem to work! These activities can be "canned" and streamed for viewing by students in independent study mode.

Even if one's course design or the available technology precludes synchronous interaction, there are still opportunities to inject more than text-based lectures and discussions into the course. Online learning provides an opportunity for the teacher to build in video or audio presentations of themselves to enhance their presence to distributed learners.

The challenge for teachers designing and organising the online learning context is to create a mix of learning activities that are appropriate to student needs, teacher skills and style, and institutional technical capacity. Doing so within the ever-present financial constraints of formal education systems is a challenge that will direct online learning design and implementation for the foreseeable future.

Task of Facilitating Discourse

The second component of teacher presence is the critical task of facilitating discourse. We use the term discourse rather than discussion, as it conveys the meaning of relating to the "the process or power of reasoning", rather than the more social connotation of conversation. Discourse not only facilitates the creation of the community of inquiry, but also is the means by which learners develop their own thought processes, through the necessity of articulating them to others.

Discourse helps students uncover misconceptions in their own thinking, or disagreements with the teacher or other students. Such conflict provides opportunity for exposure of cognitive dissonance that, from a Piagetian perspective, is critical to intellectual growth. In fulfillment of this component of teaching presence, the teacher regularly reads and responds to student contributions and concerns, constantly searching for ways to support understanding in the individual student and the development of the learning community as a whole.

The first task of the e-learning teacher is to develop a sense of trust and safety within the electronic community. In the absence of this trust, learners will feel uncomfortable and constrained in posting their thoughts and comments. We usually facilitate this trust formation by having students post a series of introductory comments about themselves. It is useful to request specific information, and to model an answer to the response request yourself. For example the e-teacher may request that students articulate their reasons for enrolling in the course or their interest in the subject matter.

Many online courses rely extensively on a model of discourse wherein the teacher posts question or discussion items relevant to readings or other forms of content dissemination. Over-reliance on this form of discourse soon becomes boring, and allows much of the learning to be focused on responding to teacherinitiated items, rather than challenging students to formulate their own questions and comments about course content. We have seen much greater levels of participation, motivation, and student satisfaction when such discussion groups are led by student moderators. However, it cannot be assumed that students have the necessary skills to undertake successful moderation of class discussion, so role modeling by the teacher for the initial discussions is usually helpful.

Online Learning Assessment

No element of course design concerns the student in a formal educational context more than that related to assessment. Effective teaching presence demands explicit and detailed discussion of the criteria on which student learning will be assessed. A teacher who cultivates a presence of flexibility, concern, and empathy will reflect these characteristics in the style and format of assessment.

We know, from researches on assessment, that timely, detailed feedback provided as near in time as possible to the performance of the assessed behavior is most effective in providing motivation and in shaping behavior and mental constructs. For this reason, machine evaluations, such as those provided in online multiplechoice test questions or in simulations, can be very effective learning devices. However, most models of online learning also stress the capacity for direct communication and feedback from teacher to the student. This feedback is provided as an integral part of the discourse facilitation function of the online teacher.

A commonly used technique in formal online education is to require students to post comments as a component of the student assessment. This practice has been hotly debated on online learning discussion lists. In their discussion of college students studying online, Jiang and Ting report that students' perceived learning was significantly correlated to the percentage of grade weight assigned to participation, and their resulting participation in discussion. However, for some, the practice of marking for participation seems only to recall the onerous practice of attendance marking that rewards the quantity and not the quality of participation.

Others counter that in the absence of incentive for participation, a community will not be created. Palloff and Pratt argue that, given the emphasis on the process of learning in a social context that defines much constructivist-based learning design, participation in the process must be evaluated and appropriately rewarded. Most online students are practical adults with much competition for their time; thus they are unlikely to participate in activities that are marginalised or viewed as supplemental to the course goals and assessment schema. Student assessment of any kind requires that the teacher be explicit, fair, consistent, and as objective as possible. The following examples illustrate how two experienced online learning teachers assess participation, and thereby enhance their own teaching presence.

Susan Levine has developed a very clear set of instructions that describes her expectations for student contributions to asynchronous online learning courses that she has used in graduate-level education courses. She posts the following message to her students.

1. The instructor will start each discussion by posting one or more questions at the beginning of each week. The discussion will continue until the following Sunday night, at which time the discussion board will close for that week.

2. Please focus on the questions posted. But-do bring in related thoughts and material, other readings, or questions that occur to you from the ongoing discussion.

3. You are expected to post at least two substantive messages for each discussion question. Your postings should reflect an understanding of the course material.

4. Your postings should advance the group's negotiation of ideas and meanings about the material; that is, your contributions should go beyond a "ditto." Some ways you can further the discussion include:

   - expressing opinions or observations. These should be offered in depth and supported by more than personal opinion.
   - making a connection between the current discussion and previous discussions, a personal experience, or concepts from the readings,
   - commenting on or asking for clarification of another student's statement,
   - synthesising other students' responses, or
   - posing a substantive question aimed at furthering the group's understanding.

Notice how these instructions guide studenis on both the quantity and the quality of contributions expected. Levine then goes onto to describe qualitative aspects of a substantive posting. Notice also the "teaching presence" that emerges from this posting of requirements. Levine reveals her teaching presence as structured and explicit, yet appreciative of qualitative outcomes associated with deep learning and critical thinking.

Nada Dabbagh, from George Mason University, offers a slightly more prescriptive set of recommendations for posting.

- Postings should be evenly distributed during the discussion period.
- Postings should be a minimum of one short paragraph and a maximum of two paragraphs.
- Avoid postings that are limited to "I agree" or "great idea," etc. If you agree with a posting then say why you agree by supporting your statement with concepts from the readings or by bringing in a related example or experience.
- Address the questions as much as possible.
- Try to use quotes from the articles that support your postings.

Include page numbers when you do that.

- Build on others' responses to create threads.
- Bring in related prior knowledge.
- Use proper etiquette.

Table 1 shows Dabbagh's sample framework for assessing messages on a weekly basis. Note that one of the protocols is the use of proper etiquette, including language, typing, and spelling. The imposition of a requirement to adhere to particular protocols or standards is a hotly contested question among elearning teachers.

Table 1. Evaluation criteria for facilitating an online/class discussion

Criterion	Excellent	Good	Average	Poor
Timely discussion contributions	5-6 postings well distributed throughout the week	4-6 postings distributed throughout the week	3-6 postings somewhat distributed	2-6 not distributed throughout the week
Responsiveness to discussion and demonstration of knowledge and understanding gained from assigned reading	very clear that readings were understood and incorporated well into responses	readings were understood and incorporated into responses	postings have questionable relationship to reading material	not evident that readings were understood and/or not incorporated into discussion
Adherence to online protocols	all online protocols followed	1 online protocol not adhered to	2-3 online protocols not adhered to	4 or more online protocols not adhered to
Points	9-10	8	6-7	5 or less

Some suggest that new forms of expression, grammar, and even spelling are arising in this medium, and that the lack of common tools that plague many conferencing systems should allow for a much more relaxed form of expression. Others argue that requiring high standard of written communication helps students learn to communicate effectively in the online learning academic context. Notice how Dabbagh requires more frequent posting than Levine, and further stipulates that the messages should be spread through the week. The second set of criteria illustrates the way the online discussion is used to motivate students to complete the weekly readings. Finally, the adherence to a list of online protocol categories links grading explicitly to quantitatively measurable student behaviors.

Both of the above instruction and marking schemes provide extremely valuable guidance to learners and make clear and explicit the requirements of the teacher. But what are the costs of such evaluation? Assuming 20-30 students in an online learning class, the weekly assessment proscribed by Dabbagh could be a very time consuming activity. The amount of time required for assessment depends, in part, on the tools available to the online teacher.

A good online learning system facilitates the display of the weekly postings by each student. An exemplary system would incorporate a number of active teacher agents that would:

- scan the postings for spelling and grammatical errors.
- total the number of words.
- allow the display of preceding or subsequent postings and the location of the posting in its thread to help assess "responsiveness."

- graph the posting dates to allow quick visual identification of the timeliness of each contribution.
- present a grade book for easy entry of weekly scores.
- when appropriate, provide assistance for the teacher to create and automatically mark a variety of multiple choice, matching, and fill-in-the-blank type questions for student self assessment.
- automatically alert students when a grade has been posted or altered.

Finally, it should be noted that creating a teaching presence is a challenging and rewarding task, but cannot be a life-consuming one. Research on assessment in distance education has shown that rapid feedback is important for both understanding and motivation to complete courses. However, the instantaneous nature of online learning can lead to an unrealistic expectation by learners that teachers will provide instant feedback and assessment on submitted assignments.

The virtual teacher has to lead a real life, so setting and adhering to appropriate timelines helps students hold realistic expectations and relieves the teacher of the unrealistic expectation of providing instantaneous, 24-hour-a-day feedback. In addition, online learning teachers must become ruthless time managers, guarding against the tendency to check online activity constantly, and to do everything to support the learners that can be done, rather than everything that can be done within the constraints of a busy professional and personal life. Some online teachers, especially those teaching at graduate levels, may be uncomfortable with the prescriptive nature of the guidelines presented above. These teachers are often more comfortable with subjective assessments of student contributions to the online community and demonstration of their individual learning.

This type of assessment presents challenges to both students and teachers as a result of the subjective nature of the assessment and the time required to review all contributions made during a course in order to assign a grade. For these reasons, a number of authors have written about ways in which the student's own postings can be used as the basis for student assessment.

Typically, these self-reflective assessments require students at the end of the course to illustrate both their contributions and evidence of learning by composing a "reflection piece," in which they quote from their own posting to the course. They should be given guidance to help them extract quotations that illustrate their contributions. Obviously students who have not participated will not be able to provide any transcript references from their own postings, and thus, will generally receive lower evaluation scores on this project. Alternatively, a vicariously participating student (i.e., a lurker) may still be able to show learning by selective extraction of relevant postings from other students.

In summary, giving directions for and modeling effective online discourse is a critical component of creating effective teaching presence. Assigning a portion of the assessment for the class to participation is a common practice in online learning courses. If participation is to be a formal and assessed requirement of the course, then developing and implementing an explicit assessment framework are essential, but potentially time-consuming, teacher tasks.

Some online learning teachers make this assessment into a more reflective task by assigning students the task of using their posting in the class conference as evidence of their understanding of content concepts and intellectual growth during the class. This type of assessed learning activity forces students to make quality contributions, and then to reflect on them. This strategy moves the locus of responsibility from the teacher to the student, a solution that can save teacher time while contributing to student understanding and metacognition.

Direct Instruction

In this final category, teachers provide intellectual and scholarly leadership, and share their subject matter knowledge with students. The online teacher must be able to set and communicate the intellectual climate of the course, and model the qualities of a scholar, including sensitivity, integrity, and commitment to the unrelenting pursuit of truth. The students and the teacher often have expectations that the teacher will communicate content knowledge. Ideally, this knowledge is enhanced by the teacher's personal interest, excitement, and in-depth understanding of the content and its application in the context of formal study. The cognitive apprenticeship model espoused by Collins, Brown, and Newman, Rogoff's model of apprenticeship in thinking, and Vygotsky'sscaffolding analogies illustrate a helping role for teachers in providing instructional support to students from their position of greater content knowledge.

Although many authors recommend a "guide on the side" approach to teaching in e-learning, this type of laissez faire approach diminishes a fundamental component of teaching and learning in formal education. A key feature of social cognition and constructivist learning models is the participation of an adult, or expert, or more skilled peer who "scaffolds" a novice's learning. This role of the teacher involves direct instruction that makes use of the subject matter and pedagogical expertise of the teacher.

Some theorists have argued that online teaching is unlike classroom-based teaching, in that "the teacher must adopt the role of facilitator not content provider". This arbitrary distinction between facilitator and content provider is troublesome. Garrison, in a lively exchange, focused on differentiating so-called teacher-centered and studentcentered instruction, makes the point that "the self-directed assumption of andragogy suggests a high degree of independence that is often inappropriate from a support perspective and which also ignores issues of what is worthwhile or what qualifies as an educational experience".

Gilly Salmon describes the role and functions of an "emoderator." In this model, the teacher's role in online conferencing is that of facilitator of learning. Her description suggests that the emoderator does not require extensive subject matter expertise; she writes "they need a qualification at least at the same level and in the same topic as the course for which they are moderating". Such minimal subject level competency seems to be less than that expected by learners and peers in higher education settings. Anderson et al. write :

> "we believe that there are many fields of knowledge, as well as attitudes and skills, that are best learned in forms of higher education that require the active participation of a subject matter expert in the critical discourse. This subject matter expert is expected to provide direct instruction by interjecting comments, referring students to information resources, and organising activities that allow the students to construct the content in their own minds and personal contexts."

Often, students hold misconceptions that impair their capacity to build more correct conceptions and mental schemata. The design of effective learning activities leads to opportunities for students themselves to uncover these misconceptions, but the teacher's comments and questions as direct instruction are also invaluable.

Although teaching presence is most commonly set in synchronous or asynchronous activities of the virtual classroom, it can also be set through fixed formats such as access to "frequently asked questions" databases or audio-, video-, or text-based presentations. Direct instruction can also be provided through an instructor's annotations of the scholarly work of others, including reviews of articles, textbooks, or Web sites.

The teacher may be asked to provide direct instruction on technical questions about access to Net-based resources, manipulation of the networking software, operation of other tools or resources, and other technical concerns related to effective use of subject related resources.

Cecreating a Virtual Presence

Salmon has developed a model for e-moderators that demarcates the progression of tasks that the online teacher moves through in the process of effectively moderating an online course. The process begins with providing students with access and motivation. In this stage, any technical or social issues that inhibit participation are addressed, and students are encouraged to share information about themselves to create a virtual presence. In the second stage, Salmon suggests that the emoderator continues to develop online socialisation by "building bridges between cultural, social and learning environments". In the third stage, referred as "information exchange," Salmon suggests that the teaching task moves to facilitating learning tasks, moderating content-based discussions, and bringing to light student misconceptions and misunderstandings. In the fourth stage, that of "knowledge construction," students focus on creating knowledge artifacts and projects that collaboratively and individually illustrate their understanding of course content and approaches. In the final "development" stage, learners become responsible for their own learning and that of their group by creating final projects, working on summative assignments, and demonstrating achievement of learning outcomes.

Salmon's model provides a useful guide and planning tool for online learning teachers, however it should not be considered prescriptive. For example, students may be entering the online class with a great deal of technical and social experience of the online learning environment. In such cases, technical and social issues may have been resolved some time ago. Alternatively, a heterogeneous group may have some very sophisticated and experienced students, and some novices new to the online learning environment. Busy adult students may be anxious to avoid what they see as unproductive "ice breakers" associated with Stages 1 and 2, and to proceed to more content rich and potentially more meaningful learning activities associated with later stages. Thus, Salmon's model must be customised to the unique needs of each online learning community.

Qualities of Online Teachers

First and primarily, an excellent e-teacher is an excellent teacher. They like dealing with learners; they have sufficient knowledge of their subject domain; they can convey enthusiasm both for the subject and for their task as a learning motivator; and they are equipped with a pedagogical understanding of the learning process, and have a set of learning activities at their disposal by which to orchestrate, motivate, and assess effective learning.

Beyond these generic teaching skills is a second set of technical skills. One does not have to be a technical expert to be an effective online teacher. However, one must have sufficient technical skill to navigate and contribute effectively within the online learning context, access to necessary hardware, and sufficient internet efficacy to function within the inevitable technical challenges of these new environments. Internet efficacy is a personal sense of competence and comfort in the environment, such that the need for basic troubleshooting skills does not send the teacher into terror-filled incapacity.

Finally, during this early period of creation and adoption of this new learning context, an effective online learning teacher must have the type of resilience, innovativeness, and perseverance typical of all pioneers in unfamiliar terrain.

7

Psychology of Teaching Mathematics

Psychology of mathematics teachers is an important component in teachers education and also in curriculum planning and the process of implementing the curriculum. The complicacy of teaching mathematics in classroom is due not only to teacher's personality and belief system, but also to social aspects of teacher's mathematical communication. A good source for finding important factors taking part in the social aspects of teaching mathematics can be borrowed from sociology of science. The amount of similarity between the scientific community and the process of mathematical education of students in classroom depends on how natural the process of learning is implemented by teacher.

The meaning of doing, teaching and learning mathematics varies in different classes. This variation is partially due to the perspectives of teachers towards mathematics and towards the role of teacher in education and these perspectives are affected by the their mathematical knowledge and their professional abilities as a teacher. Both of these could be strengthened by teachers education programs, but promotion of the level of abstractness of teacher's knowledge and his/her professional abilities takes time and is not easily achieved. Therefore, not every teacher could teach every style. We have to introduce different models for a mathematics classroom, so that different teachers with different levels of sophistication in teaching could find a model appropriate for their professional capacities.

Teacher as a Source of Information

Knowledge in such a classroom is nothing but row information and teaching and learning are nothing but transformation and communication of information. Teacher either orally explains the information to the class or writes the information on board or shows students demonstrations on computer or on data show. Some other information are made available to students by handing them books and papers.

Student's access to information is not always in full detail. Most of the time teacher chooses the key information and makes it known to his/her pupils. Teacher also gives some explanations on the meaning and the relations between the packages of information. This role of such a teacher could be easily played by computers. Information technology could provide students with more detailed, accurate, advanced, and accessible information.

The role of student in such a class is taking notes and trying to memorise them. Repetition helps students to keep information in mind for a longer period of time. Decisions that a teacher should make in such a classroom are very formal and can be modeled to be performed by a computer. Teacher decides about the language and tools which each piece of information shall be demonstrated to the class, and also the exercises which help students internalise the information. Teacher has to choose the key information and decide about appropriate references to introduce students for further study. Teacher has to decide about how to assess a piece of information too. We shall introduce models for different personalities of teachers in making such decisions.

Teacher as a Coach

In this classroom, teacher is trying to discover his/her students personal talents and train them in direction of perfection of these talents. The particular characteristics of the mathematical knowledge being discussed in class has an important role in this training. Teacher makes determining decisions in choosing the material to be discussed in class. Different examples demonstrated in class are aimed to train different groups of students of different talents. Teacher shall be able to teach students the particular practices and exercises which help them in perfection of their talents. Teacher supports and protects his/her students in the storm of their mental contradictions. He/she has to provide an appropriate atmosphere in classroom for treatment of students mental contradictions.

The role of student in this classroom is doing mathematics. Student personally gets actively involved in enrichment of his/her knowledge up to a level in which he/she be able to overcome mental contradictions leaning on his/her own personal abilities. Students also cooperate with teacher in the process of discovery of their talents. Teacher has to introduce a classification of mathematical talents and decide about the manners in which these talents show off so that he/she can decide about talents of students and exercises which can lead students to perfection of their talents. Teacher has to decide about different levels of student access to each of these talents.

TEACHER AS A ROLE MODEL

In this classroom various forms of mathematical knowledge are discussed. Teacher tries to openly demonstrate the process of thinking to the class. Students could learn how to solve problems, only if they can openly watch their teacher wrestle with hard problems. Teacher must be able to think loudly so that students could imitate his/her skills of problem solving. Teacher could serve as a good role model, only if students can watch his/her thoughts inside out. In this classroom, teacher shall do mathematics which is not familiar with, in front of the students. Teacher tries to make students involved in his/her process of problem solving. If this role could be successfully played in classroom, students have been given the best possible education for group thinking. A teacher for this class should be very experienced and knowledgeable in mathematics.

The role of students in such a classroom is doing mathematics while keeping the teacher in mind as a role model. Students are able to construct their mathematical abilities personally and guide the direction of progress in their mental skills. Most of the decisions that such a teacher should make are personal decisions which he/she makes in problem solving and the class is supposed to imitate him in making personal decisions.

TEACHER AS A LIFE COMPANION

In this classroom, teacher tries to apply mathematics to students everyday life situations. To this teacher, knowledge is what is practically useful. Teacher tries to introduce mathematics as a human endeavour. The aim of teacher is to translate problems of everyday life situations to the abstract language of mathematics and solve them using mathematical machinery and then translate the solution back to the language of everyday life. This ability should be internalised in students so that they use their mathematical skills outside school. In such a class, the human history of evolution of mathematical concepts is under focus. Also, the process of discovery in problem solving should be recorded carefully by students. Strategies of problem solving and skills of decision making in course of discovery are taught carefully in this classroom.

Students engage in groups in solving everyday life problems using mathematics. Learning is a group activity but each student has a particular interest and perspective in doing mathematics. Every student helps his/her colleagues during the learning process and takes advantage of the helps offered by other colleagues. Teacher has to decide about different skills that students should learn and about different levels of sophistication in these skills. Teacher has to decide about the skills which each of the students could learn better by having a classification of students learning strategies.

Teacher as a Scientist

In this classroom, teacher unveils the mathematical order of the universe we live in. For this teacher, mathematical knowledge is based on ideas borrowed from nature. Teacher makes sure his/her students learn to observe nature, discover mathematical ideas from it and use them in development of mathematics. History of science is under focus. Students should learn how mathematical ideas taken from nature have affected human civilisation. Proposing reasonable conjectures base on scientific methodology is an important skill which students should learn. The aim of teacher is not only familiarising students with applications of mathematics to other branches of science, but also teaching them skills of discovering new applications of mathematics to other areas of science. These applications do influence the practice of scientists in other areas.

Students in such a classroom search in groups for mathematical ideas in nature. They recognise mathematics as the language of nature and try to get a better understanding of nature through this language. Student also tries to apply mathematics to other branches of science. Teacher has to decide about how he/she can motivate students to become interested in nature and its order. Teacher has to decide about the branches of science that a student is fascinated by, so that he/she could insert mathematical ideas to teach the student how to apply mathematics in basic different branches of science.

Teacher as a Philosopher

In this classroom, mathematics is an abstract knowledge independent of nature which is governed by the mathematical essence of the world of creation. Mathematical ideas could be borrowed not only from nature, but also from beyond. Teacher tries to discover the mathematical order with the aim of demonstrating his/her students unity in the essence of creation. Teacher tries to find similar ideas in different parts of mathematics and use them to unveil the unity beyond these ideas. In such a class, the abstract science of mathematics is formulated independent of nature. Mathematics has many abstract layers and teacher tries to connects these layers by unifying different mathematical theories in each layer. This is a new perspective to learning mathematics in which each student does mathematics in a particular layer of abstractness.

Student tries to structure the abstract mathematical nature of his/her mind and is interested in knowing the essence beyond the mathematical ideas. Relating different branches of mathematics and performing computations and comparing them in different branches are tools which students use to extend the abstract structure of their mind. Learning and doing mathematics is no longer possible in groups because of the high level of abstractness of this kind of mathematical activity. Student is learning mathematics for reasons beyond mathematics. So, again the particular mathematical content of mathematics does not play any important role in such a classroom.

In such a classroom, teacher has to decide about the particular level of abstractness each student could handle. Teacher also has to make sure if unification of a few different examples and creation of a more abstract generalisation has actually occurred for a particular student. Teacher has to have a personal knowledge of different layers of abstractness and be able to decide each particular mathematical content belongs to which of these abstract layers. Teacher chooses a particular mathematical content which he/she is most familiar with its abstract layers.

Teacher as a Physician

In such a classroom, teacher is trying to give special treatments to the minds of his/her students. For this kind of teacher, knowledge is only used as a means of communication in order to get information on how students think. A teacher tries to replace an unorganised mind by an ordered healthy mind. This is why he/she demonstrates some examples of truthful deductions and accurate reasoning to the class.

The main occupation of the teacher in this classroom, is discovering the mental weaknesses of students and trying to bring them to a normal position in which all of their different abilities demonstrate a coherent progress during the process of mathematical education. Only a very well-trained experienced teacher can play this role in the classroom. There is some chance that some day a detailed classification of learner's behaviour plus a well developed theory of information engineering could partially replace the role of these teachers in the educational system.

In this classroom, students try to awaken the abilities of their mind, by learning and imitating examples of deductions and reasoning presented in class. They try to cooperate with their teacher in discovering their mental weaknesses. Teacher has to have a classification of human mathematical mind so that he/she can decide each student belongs to which class and then comparing student's abilities with the particular class he/she has chosen, decide about weaknesses and strength of the student. Classification of weaknesses is an abstract procedure, because abnormal situations are exceptions; but teacher has to put similar ones in the same class, so that he/she be able to study them by their symptoms.

IMPACTS OF TEACHERS' PERSONALITY

Many different decisions has to be made by teachers and the examples we have already mentioned is by no means a complete list. Nor is the different models we introduced for a mathematics classroom. Therefore, we shall find a way in which mathematical modelling of the personality of teachers in decision making be independent of the particular decisions that they have to make. Otherwise classification of their behaviour in class would be a complicated task. To do this, we shall focus on the social aspects of learning. This will help us to understand the personality of the teacher independent of the particular meaning of learning in different classes.

Learning mathematics and problem solving in classroom has a completely different nature from individual attempts in doing mathematics. When working in groups, not only decision making in different stages of problem solving is influenced by group discussions, but also diversity of perspectives towards the solution of the problem smoothens the process of individual learning. Human forms of communication makes the process of learning and its content to be considered in more human perspectives. For example, mathematical arguments instead of being considered as abstract human independent truth, seem like an address which is directing our mind to a particular place.

Different addresses could lead to the same conclusions and at the end, the new places discovered are of main importance, not the particular nature of the addresses leading to that place. In better words, different minds could be satisfied with arguments of different natures. Students eventually develop different personalities in accepting arguments and the teacher will not be able to force them to think the same about the truth of a mathematical proposition. Teacher can only focus on skills of students in applying the mathematics they learn to different aspects of their life.

Management of Maths Learning

Management of learning in a classroom is very similar to management of development of science in a scientific society. Different social aspects of science, could be regarded as different aspects of group learning in classroom, and the teacher has to make decisions about each of these aspects for the good of his/her students learning. Teacher's decision making is affected by many external factors. Here we mention a few of them:

- The mathematical subject which is to be discussed could have numerical, geometric, algebraic or analytic nature. This could cause different decisions of teacher in his/her particular approach in teaching the subject matter.
- Students motivation in learning mathematics could be of many different levels of abstractness. Students with different motivations could not be treated the same and this affects the process of teacher's decision making.
- Different learning strategies of students, and their particular mental process of thinking calls for different educational treatments and different styles of teaching mathematics. Efficient decision making of teachers could cause a more fruitful education for each of student's minds.
- The goals and points of view of the educational system towards mathematical education of students force limitations in the teachers personality in educating students. They have to follow a predetermined path in developing students mathematical skills.
- The particular shape and direction of historical movement of the educational system which is not personal, and is headed forward, reducing the value of previous systems, forces the teachers to keep themselves up to date in their teaching style and personality in decision making in classroom.

- The particular mother tongue of students and the scientific language in which the subject matter is being discussed, affects teachers decision making as a means of communication. The scientific language is usually internationalised but has to be made compatible with the mother tongue of students. Students learning mathematics in second language has to get particular educational treatment which affects the teaching personality of educators.
- The social hierarchy of the mathematically educated, for example engineers, affects the perspective of students towards mathematics and directly affect the teaching personalities of mathematics teachers.
- The social role of mathematics in the society which is changed by time does affect the practical meaning of mathematics in classroom and in term could cause affections in mathematics teachers decision making.
- The actual sites of learning and practising mathematics like schools, universities, research institutes, government organisations, and their scientific structure defines a mathematical culture which affects the ways teachers decide in classroom.
- The social human personality of a mathematics teacher or a mathematician also puts limitations on mathematics teachers behaviour in classroom, which in turn affects their educational decision making.

Development of Mathematical Knowledge

Under all the above mentioned limitations and governing rules, the process of teachers decision making is aimed towards development of mathematical knowledge in classroom. In order to gain a better knowledge of the social structure of students scientific progress, the essential factors of development of science in society could be modeled in a mathematics classroom. The history of development of science contains detailed information about the social structure of scientific progress. Here we list a few important factors which teachers could regard as the subject of decision making in mathematics classroom.

- *Distinction of social and mental roles of students:* Teachers shall try to distinguish the role of each student in group learning. Also the particular mental habits and learning schemes of all students shall be made clear to them. The philosophical and scientific aspects of the mathematical subject matter shall also be separated. Each of these distinctions supports the development of mathematical knowledge in classroom.

- *Structural values:* Many of the modern values in classroom plays an efficient role in progress of group learning. Valuing rationalism against traditionalism, liberalism against authoritarianism, getting actively involved against inactive indifference, equity against injustice, supports development of different components of knowledge in classroom.

- *Instrumental needs:* Many students have instrumental perspectives towards learning and gaining knowledge. The environment around them, and opportunities available to them makes them have opportunistic motivations for learning. Teacher can use these instrumental motivations to guide the process of group learning in classroom.

- *Economical factors:* One may think that economical motivations for development of science contradicts the innocence and purity of science. But modern history of science has shown that if a modest budget be available to the teachers, they can use the money for the well-being of the education of their students. Making right decisions about economical issues could help the process of learning.

- *Political structures and needs:* Financial matters and issues of school politics usually have the tendency to combine in affecting the education of students. School has political needs and would be happy to get support from its students in this direction. Matters of politics could be directed by teacher to motivate improvement of mathematical knowledge in classroom.
- *Religion*: In every society, values and religion have a very close relationship. A religion that its values supports the progress of science could be used in guiding the classroom. It shall be pointed out that religion and science have a complicated relationship which could be contradictory in many societies. Using religion as a motivation is a complicated and delicate art that only few teachers are capable of.
- *The social structure of classroom:* In case development of group thinking in classroom be emphasised in an educational system, and particular social structures could be engineered in classroom to support development of mathematical knowledge, teacher can guide students education by making correct decisions in engineering the working groups and the ways in which they scientifically communicate.
- *Mathematical modelling of social decision making:* All of the above factors are ways in which a teacher can motivate a social behaviour. What the teacher has to decide about is if an action will have the effect he/she expects and if his/her decision will find social ground.

The easiest way is trial and error and gaining experience about the social behaviour of students in a society. But this is not an efficient way, since in this period of time, social structures are under constant construction and development. Experiences that a teacher gains soon will be useless because of social evolutions. So every teacher has a mental model which he/she uses for prediction of social behaviour of students. If we could approximate teachers mental models with mathematical models, such mathematical models not only could replace the experience of teachers, but also would give information about decision making of teachers for different generations. One could predict the social behaviour of students via these mathematical models and make decisions according to one's predictions.

Teachers have different mental models, because they have different philosophies for a social phenomena taking shape. It is these different philosophies which shall be the subject of our field study. Here we list a few perspectives which is by no means a complete list:

Philosophy of influential individuals: Many teachers believe that classroom is socially following a few influential individuals. These individuals could be the teacher of a few students. According to this philosophy, a group behaviour in classroom is accepted by students, only if a few influential individuals follow it. Teachers who believe this philosophy try to be influential in classroom, or at least influential of the social leaders of students among them. Sometimes they try to choose individuals and make them role models, so that they become influential in time.

Mathematical modelling of this system is very easy. It is enough to record the actions of students and discover which of the students show influential social roles in classroom.

- *Philosophy of majority:* This philosophy suggests that classroom follows the majority. If the majority of the students are prepared to accept a social behaviour in classroom, the minority will follow them. In order to predict the social behaviour in such a classroom, teacher has to be familiar with many of the students so that he/she could predict individual reactions of students to the social behaviour. For mathematical modelling of this system, one can decide if the majority accepts a social change, by asking students to fill a questionnaire which shows students particular opinions in this regard.

- *Philosophy of coherence of social structures:* According to this philosophy, the classroom follows the dominant global social structures outside the classroom. Teachers following this philosophy try to model the social behaviour they want to suggest to the classroom, in the global society and try to verify if it will find social ground or not.

  Mathematical modelling of this kind of decision making is going to be very difficult. Because a natural dictionary between the social phenomena in classroom and social equivalents in the outside society does not exist. One shall make the task of decision making very abstract in order to find an equivalent form of it, in the outside society.

- *Philosophy of social evolution in time:* Some teachers believe that if one is supposed to guide the students towards predetermined goals, very rarely the classroom is naturally prepared to move in the direction suggested by the teacher. In fact, a social change should occur so that the teacher be able to guide the classroom to new social order. But social change is a continuous slow process which takes time and constant supervision. In this philosophy decision making is a long term process.

Mathematical modelling of this system of decision making is possible if the teacher can list a few behavioural goals for the changes he/she suggests. Then constant recording of instances that these behaviours are shown in classroom, can give us information on the extent to which the classroom has had progress in achieving the behavioural goals.

– *Philosophy of social character:* Following this philosophy is an abstract practice. Some teachers believe that one can regard the classroom as a whole and define characters for the classroom as one defines a character for an individual. In fact one is modelling the society by an individual. Teacher in the process of making decisions, considers the abstract individual in his/her mind and tries to predict this individual's reaction towards the social suggestions. Then he/she translates back this behaviour to the social language of classroom. This intuitive abstract process is very hard to be modeled by a mathematical system. Because it is not at all mathematically clear in which ways a society is similar to an individual.

Curriculum Planning

As one can see from the above different personalities of teachers, there is no way that a curriculum could plan for a single model of mathematics teacher. But what can be done, is to implement a social structure in classroom for which every teacher could easily communicate socially with this structure and guide the process of development of mathematical knowledge in classroom. On the other hand, the implemented social structure on classroom should not cause limitations on the social character of classroom. Because such un-natural limitations make the structure unacceptable to students.

The curriculum should stress on coherence of the social structure of the classroom, in a way that the social system could be approximated by the character of an individual as close as possible. This approach seems natural because character of an individual is in its own right, a superposition of internal personalities which communicate inside the individual's personality.

Curriculum planning and educational system can support the coherence of the social structure of the classroom by insisting on the growth and complicacy of the social structure of the classroom. More precisely, the more the social structure of the classroom becomes advanced and mature, the more coherence between the subsystems of the classroom is implemented. The easy way, is to try to model the whole social structure of the global society inside the classroom. But this way, educational system looses ground in influencing the global social structure, which is one of the main roles that a pioneer educational system should play in the society.

Constructivism in Maths Classroom

Students actively construct "their individual mathematical worlds by reorganising their experiences in an attempt to resolve their problems". The expectation is that the student's reorganised experiences form a personal mathematical structure that is more complex, more powerful, and more abstract than it was prior to the reorganisation. Teachers who implement a constructivist approach to student learning must try to "see" both their own actions/ mathematics and their students' actions/mathematics from their students' perspective.

The role of teachers and instructional activities in a constructivist classroom is to provide motivating environments that lead to mathematical problems for students to resolve. However, each student will probably find a different problem in this rich environment because each student has a different knowledge base, different experiences, and different motivations. Thus, a teacher should avoid giving problems that are "ready made".

A fundamental principle underlying the constructivist approach to learning mathematics is that a student's activity and responses are always rational and meaningful to themselves, no matter how bizarre or off-the-wall they may seem to others. One of the teacher's responsibilities is to determine or interpret the student's "rationality" and meaning. Scaffolding is a metaphor for the teacher's provision of "just enough" support to help students progress or succeed in each mathematical learning activity. Elaborating on this metaphor, Greenfield suggests: "The scaffold, as it is known in building construction, has five characteristics: it provides support, it functions as a tool; it extends the range of the worker; it allows the worker to accomplish a task not otherwise possible; and it is used selectively to aid the worker where need be.

Mathematics teachers must engage in "close listening" to each student, which requires a cognitive reorientation on their part that allows them to listen while imagining what the learning experience of the student might be like. Teachers must then act in the best way possible to further develop the mathematical experience of the student, sustain it, and modify it if necessary.

Young children enter school with a wide range of self-generated algorithms and problem solving strategies that represent their a priori conceptual understandings of mathematics. Classroom instruction too often separates the child's conceptual knowledge from the new procedures or knowledge they construct because the "students' informal ways of making meaning are given little attention".

From multiple research efforts on creating a constructivist classroom, Yackel et al. concluded that "not only are children capable of developing their own methods for completing school mathematics tasks but that each child has to construct his or her own mathematical knowledge. That is ... mathematical knowledge cannot be given to children. Rather, they develop mathematical concepts as they engage in mathematical activity including trying to make sense of methods and explanations they see and hear from others." In her survey of the research on arithmetic-based learning, Fuson concluded that students can "learn much more than is presented to them now if instruction is consistent with their thinking."

Impact of using Manipulatives

Mathematics achievement is increased through the long-term use of concrete instructional materials and that students' attitudes toward mathematics are improved when they have instruction with concrete materials provided by teachers knowledgeable about their use. Manipulative materials can:

(1) help students understand mathematical concepts and processes,

(2) increase students' flexibility of thinking,

(3) be used creatively as tools to solve new mathematical problems, and

(4) reduce students' anxiety while doing mathematics.

However, several false assumptions about the power of manipulatives are often made. First, manipulatives cannot impart mathematical meaning by themselves. Second, mathematics teachers cannot assume that their students make the desired interpretations from the concrete representation to the abstract idea. And third, the interpretation process that connects the manipulative to the mathematics can involve quite complex processing.

Students do not discover or understand mathematical concepts simply by manipulating concrete materials. Mathematics teachers need to intervene frequently as part of the instruction process to help students focus on the underlying mathematical ideas and to help build bridges from the students' work with the manipulatives to their corresponding work with mathematical symbols or actions.

Mathematics teachers need much more assistance in both how to select an appropriate manipulative for a given mathematical concept and how to help students make the necessary connections between the use of the manipulative and the mathematical concept.

Manipulatives need to be selected and used carefully, as they also can be distracting, ambiguous, and open to misinterpretation. Furthermore, if "multiple embodiments" of a mathematical concept are involved, students might have a hard time focusing on the correct interpretation. In his study of teachers as they used manipulatives in mathematics classrooms, Jackson documented the existence of these "mistaken beliefs":

1. Almost any manipulative can be used to teach any mathematical concept.
2. Manipulatives simplify the students' learning of mathematics.
3. Good mathematics teaching always includes the use of manipulatives.
4. The number of manipulatives used is positively correlated to the amount of learning that occurs.
5. Teachers should pick one multipurpose manipulative and use it to teach all or most of the mathematics.
6. Manipulatives are more useful in the primary grades than in the upper grades.
7. Manipulatives are more useful with low-ability students than high-ability students.

Teachers sometimes overestimate the value of manipulatives because they as adults are able to "see" the mathematical concepts or processes being represented. Children do not have this "adult eye". Concrete materials are likely to be misused when a teacher has in mind that students will learn to perform some prescribed activity with them. Teachers need to take into account the "contextual distance" between the manipulatives and the mathematical concept to be experienced. For example, baseten blocks represent place value concepts both physically and physically, while colored chips and money are less visual models because they have no physical features that suggest placc value relationships.

The use of concrete manipulatives do not seem as effective in promoting algebraic understanding as they are in promoting student understanding of place value and the basic computational processes. Manipulatives help students at all grade levels conceptualise geometric shapes and their properties to the extent those students can create definitions, pose conjectures, and identify general relationships.

In a survey of research on manipulatives, Suydam and Higgins concluded: "Lessons involving manipulative materials will produce greater mathematical achievement than will lessons in which manipulative materials are not used if the manipulative materials are used well" and made these suggestions:

1. Manipulatives should be used frequently and throughout the instructional program in a manner consistent with the goals of the program.
2. Manipulatives should be used in conjunction with other learning aids such as diagrams, technology, and resource texts.
3. Manipulatives should be used by students in a manner consistent with the mathematics content and the mathematics content should be adjusted to maximise the potential of the manipulatives.
4. Manipulatives should be used with learning activities that are exploratory and deductive in approach.
5. The manipulatives used should be the simplest possible and yet be the most representative of the mathematical ideas being explored.
6. Manipulatives should be used with learning activities that include the symbolic recording of results and ideas.

PROBLEMS SOLVING STRATEGIES

Middle school students respond to a word problem with one of four basic types of strategies:

1. Coping Strategies:
   a. Guess at the operation to be used.
   b. Find the numbers in the problem and add (or subtract, multiply, or divide, depending on recent classroom computational work or the operation the student is most comfortable with).
2. Computation-Driven Strategies:
   a. Look at the numbers in the word problem; they will "tell" you which operation to use
   b. Try all four operations and choose the most reasonable answer.
3. Slightly Less Immature Strategies:
   a. Look for "key" words or phrases to tell which operations to use.
   b. Decide whether the answer should be larger or smaller than the given numbers. If larger, try both addition and multiplication and choose the more reasonable answer. If smaller, try both subtraction and division and choose the more reasonable answer.
4. Desired Strategy:
   a. Choose the operation which meaning fits the story.

In addition to these strategies, the researchers made three additional conclusions. First, students of all ability levels used immature strategies at times. Gifted students often used an immature, computation-driven strategy (2b). Finally, strategy 3b was used productively by many students, with it failing them only when multipliers less than 1 were involved.

Teachers can provide several generic teaching strategies to help students solve word problems, especially when the student can transfer a known strategy for one problem category to a new problem:

1. Have students discuss carefully chosen exemplary problems and their solutions to minimise gaps in their understandings of the intermediate steps.
2. Ask students to focus on each problem's conditions and the effects of the subsequent solution steps.
3. Help students organise their solution steps into a hierarchically organised goal structure.
4. Encourage students to label parts of the solution process (as subgoals) as it is implemented.
5. Challenge students to reflect on and discuss alternate routes to a solution.

Drawing diagrams to represent a problem does facilitate a student's search for a "relevant" solution for the problem.

Students have difficulty representing and solving algebraic word problems because they rely on a direct syntax approach which involves a "phrase-by-phrase" translation of the problem into a variable equation.

Fuson et al. proposed a research-based framework that unifies the mathematics curriculum and the teaching/ learning process. It incorporates the different cognitive phases that students should pass through when solving word problems:

1. *Building a situation conception:* The students' focus is on understanding the vocabulary used, understanding the meaning of each sentence, and integrating all of these meanings to understand the problem situation-a good teaching strategy is to ask students to retell the problem in their own words or draw a picture to illustrate the problem.

2. *Forming a mathematical conception:* The students' focus is on the numbers, the unknown(s), and building a representation of the situation using mathematical operations-a good teaching strategy is to ask students to model the situation with concrete manipulatives or diagrams.

3. *Formulating a solution method conception*: The students' focus is on the unknown(s) and the steps needed to determine the values of the unknown(s)-a good teaching strategy is to ask students to discuss their solution plans, the connections they have found in the solution process, and the methods they could use to check the reasonableness of their results.

Students, confronted with a word problem, experience cognitive difficulty if the operation required for the solution procedure is opposite to the operation in the problem's underlying structure. Other factors that create cognitive difficulty are the position of the question in the word problem, the degree of specifics in the wording of the problem, the size of the numbers, the amount of "action cueing" of the operation used in the solution, and the availability of concrete manipulatives. Attempts to determine relationships between reading ability and the ability to solve word problems have been inconsistent and inconclusive at best. Educators' assumptions regarding a connection are reasonable but not supported by the research. The one consistent factor is reading comprehension skills.

Algebra teachers should be aware that word problems that can be solved without algebra (i.e., with arithmetic) can be counterproductive. Rather, algebra students should be given problems that "discourage the search for arithmetic solutions," a search process on the teacher's part that can be as simple as changing the whole numbers in word problems to decimals.

Meaningful instruction and drill go together as part of a successful learning experience, but meaningful instruction must precede drill or practice. A balanced approach to both is needed in mathematics classrooms, as students who can access both memorised and meaningful ideas in mathematics achieve at a higher level than those who rely on either one without the other.

Synthesising both his research and other related research, Davis produced these guiding principles for using drill of number facts in a productive manner:

1. Students should not try to memorise a number fact that they do not understand.
2. Students should participate in drill knowing that the goal is to memorise facts that they understand.
3. Teachers need to emphasise remembering, not explaining, during drill sessions.
4. Teachers need to keep drill sessions brief yet include them on a daily basis.
5. Students should focus on only a few facts at a time, while also reviewing previously memorised facts.
6. Teachers need to express confidence in each student's ability to memorise all of the number facts.

7. Students should receive immediate feedback.
8. Teachers need to stress that the two key aspects of facts recall are accuracy and speed.
9. Teachers need to vary drill activities and be enthusiastic during the activity.
10. Teachers need to praise students on their progress in memorising facts, keeping a record of their individual progress.

Practice toward mastery of basic skills and procedural algorithms should not occur until students develop the meaning underlying those skills or algorithms. Research results (and frustrated teachers) consistently suggest that if this practice occurs too soon for a student, it is very difficult for that student to step back and focus on the meaning that should have been developed at the very beginning.

Students trying to master the basic addition facts should be given experiences with the derived fact strategies. For example, 5+6 can be transformed into [5+5]+1, which can be solved by the sum of the easier double [5+5]=10 and 1. Because this strategy builds on a student's number sense and meaningful relationships between basic combinations, it improves fact recall and provides a "fall-back" mechanism for students.

Students have conceptual trouble with the zero and one multiplication facts and often resort to rote memory. The difficulty perhaps is due to interference created by a dependence on the repeated-addition model for multiplication. Students need to master the basic facts and practice algorithmic procedures. The more efficiently a procedure is executed, the more mental effort that is saved to focus on other related tasks. However, such mastery and practice does not seem to contribute to the development of meaning of the underlying mathematics.

IMPACT OF COMPUTING TECHNOLOGIES

In a recent study of the long-term effect of young children's use of calculators, Groves and Stacey formed these conclusions:

1. Students will not become reliant on calculator use at "the expense of their ability to use other methods of computation."
2. Students who learn mathematics using calculators have higher mathematics achievement than noncalculator students-both on questions where they can choose any tool desired and on mental computation problems.
3. Students who learn mathematics using calculators demonstrate a significantly better understanding of negative numbers, place value in large numbers, and especially decimals.
4. Students who learn mathematics using calculators perform better at interpreting their answers, especially again with decimals.

Calculators can successfully help introduce basic concepts of algebra through extensive explorations with numerical computations. In a study of students using calculators while learning calculus, Gimmestad concluded that:

1. Students sometimes change their solution approaches because of their access to calculators.
2. Students using calculators are more effective when exploring ideas or solution approaches within a problem context.
3. Students using calculators are much more likely to check their work by retracing steps.

4. Students using calculators achieve overall at the same level as students without calculators.

Calculators enhance student's (1) use of deductive reasoning, (2) ability to elaborate retrospectively on their strategies, (3) use of specific problem solving techniques to reach successful solutions, and (4) ability to evaluate their progress while solving problems.

Calculator-using students outperform noncalculator-using students on calculatorneutral tests. Great care and rigor must be used in preparing items for such tests to ensure that the intended mathematical objectives are being assessed; it may even be necessary to norm the scores for the two groups independently. Reviewing research on the impact of calculator use in the mathematics classroom, Wheatley and Shumway et al. jointly concluded:

1. Students using calculators experience a far greater number and variety of mathematical concepts and computations.
2. Students weak in their recall of basic facts become more successful as problem solvers when given access to calculators.
3. Students using calculators express more confidence when attacking mathematical problems.
4. Students using calculators exhibit more exploratory behaviors when solving mathematical problems.
5. Students using calculators spend more time on attacking problems and less time on computing.
6. Student and teacher attitudes toward mathematics improve when calculator use becomes part of the classroom routine.

Students using graphing calculators in a precalculus class tend to perform better on critical thinking measures than those students not using calculators. Gender differences in performance on graphing tasks tend to disappear in college algebra classes when students use graphing calculators.

Graphing calculators change the nature of classroom interactions and the role of the teacher, prompting more student discussions with the teachers playing the role of consultants. Graphing calculators facilitate algebraic learning in several ways. First, graphical displays under the student's control provide insights into problem solving. Second, graphical displays paired with the appropriate questions serve as assessments of student reasoning at different levels.

Computer environments impact student attitudes and affective responses to instruction in algebra and geometry. In addition to changing the social context associated with traditional instruction, computer access provides a mechanism for students to discover their own errors, thereby removing the need for a teacher as an outside authority.

Students learn more advanced mathematics in less time and with enhanced conceptual understanding in a symbolic-manipulative computer environment. Computer environments can help students overcome statistical misconceptions because students control the important variables as they watch a sampling process or manipulate histograms. Students need experiences with computer simulations, computer spreadsheets, and data analysis programs if they are to improve their understanding of probability and statistics. Yerushalmy et al. investigated the impact of rich geometric environments created on a computer and made these conclusions:

1. Students of all ability levels can conceptualise the construction of a geometric figure in dynamic terms and accept it as a general prototype.
2. Students have trouble making conjectures based on their explorations or data.
3. Students do not think it is necessary to justify their generalisations from a finite number of cases.

Students learning in a computer environment and related algebra curriculum perform better on mathematical modeling tasks, general problem solving tasks, and even tasks involving standard algebra manipulations.

Dynamic geometry software programs create rich environments that enhance students' communications using mathematics and help students build connections between different mathematical ideas. Interactive computing technologies enhance both the teaching and learning of mathematics. Great benefits occur if the technology's power (1) is controllable by either the students or teachers, (2) is easily accessible in a way that enables student explorations, and (3) promotes student generalisations.

Graphing calculators produce data tables that help students explore meaningful problem environments prior to the learning of standard algebraic techniques. The end result is the students' enhanced understanding of the dynamics of change and the meaning underlying algebraic expressions.

Students using graphing tools on a calculator or a computer have trouble with scaling when studying functions and their graphs. A common misconception is that changes in scale also change the values on the graph, with students unaware that the real change is their perception of the graph or the amount of the graph visible on the screen.The power of calculators and computers make "the organisation and structure of algebra problematic." Easy access to graphic representations and symbolic manipulators reduce the need to manipulate algebraic expressions or to solve algebraic equations.

Graphing options on calculators provide dynamic visual representations that act as "conceptual amplifiers" for students learning algebra. Student performance on traditional algebra tasks is improved, especially relative to the development of related ideas such as transformations or invariance.

Culture of Mathematics Classroom

Multiple studies of the culture of the mathematics classroom have concluded that the student's role and actions depend primarily on the view of mathematics projected by the teacher. Teachers with an integrated, conceptual understanding of mathematics tend to organise their classrooms and learning activities that encourage students to engage and interact with the conceptual aspects of mathematics. Furthermore, the depth of the mathematics taught correlates highly with the depth of the teachers' mathematical knowledge.

Teachers maintain student engagement at doing mathematics at a high level if they (1) select appropriate tasks for the student, (2) support proactively the student's activity, (3) ask students consistently to provide meaningful explanations of their work and reasoning, (3) push students consistently to make meaningful connections, and (4) do not reduce the complexity/cognitive demands of the task. Student engagement in mathematical activities declines if teachers (1) remove the challenging aspects of the tasks, (2) shift the students' focus from understanding to either the correctness or completeness of an answer, or (3) do not allow an appropriate amount of time for students to complete the task.

A crucial role of the teacher is to structure a pervasive norm in the classroom that helping one's peers to learn is not a marginal activity, but is a central element of students' roles. In a review of 80 research studies on grouping in mathematics classrooms, Davidson concluded that students working in small groups significantly outscored students working individually in more than 40 percent of the studies. Students working as individuals in a mathematics classroom performed better in only two of the studies.

Learning mathematics in cooperative groups is effective, especially for younger students. When students reach high school, the research evidence is less clear, as these students exhibit stronger individual motivations, interact socially in more complex ways, and often are defensive or embarrassed about their knowledge and learning in mathematics.

Teachers can maximise mathematical learning in a small group environment by engaging students in learning activities that promote questioning, elaboration, explanation, and other verbalisations in which they can express their ideas and through which the group members can give and receive feedback. Students solving mathematical problems in small groups invokes three features that enhance the individual student's cognitive (re)organisation of mathematics:

1. The student experiences "challenge and disbelief" on the part of the other members of the group, which forces them to examine their own beliefs and strategies closely.

2. The group collectively provides background information, skills, and connections that a student may not have or understand.

3. The student might internalise some of the group's problem solving approaches and make them part of their personal approach.

Teachers trying to build and sustain mathematical discourse amongst students need to create an environment in which students build a "personal relationship" with mathematics. Three key elements need to be in this environment:

1. Students need to engage in authentic mathematical inquiries.
2. Students must act like mathematicians as they explore ideas and concepts.
3. Students need to negotiate the meanings of, and the connections among, these mathematical ideas with other students in the class.

Several factors influence or maintain student engagement at the level necessary to do quality mathematics. The primary factors are: high-quality tasks that build on students' prior knowledge of mathematics, effective scaffolding on the teachers' part, an appropriate amount of time to engage in the mathematics, both teacher and student modeling of high performance actions, and a sustained effort by the teacher to ask for explanations and meaning.

Several teacher actions help establish a classroom culture that supports mathematical discourse:

1. Have a routine of setting norms for both small-group and large-group activities.
2. Address student and group expectations in class.

3. Insist that students solve personally challenging problems.
4. Insist that students explain their personal solutions to peers.
5. Insist that students listen to and try to make sense of the explanations of others.
6. Insist that students try to reach consensus about solutions to a problem.
7. Insist that students resolve any conflicting interpretations or solutions.
8. Capitalise on specific incidents when a student's activity either "instantiated or transgressed a social norm" by rediscussing the classroom expectations.

Teacher' and Students' Attitudes

A student's attitude toward mathematics is not a one-dimensional construct. Just as there are different types of mathematics, there potentially are a variety of attitudes towards each type of mathematics. Despite inconsistent definitions of attitude relative to mathematics, Fennema suggests that research supports these "tentative conclusions":

1. A significant positive correlation exists between student attitudes and mathematics achievement-this relationship increases as students proceed through the grades.
2. Student attitudes toward mathematics are quite stable.
3. The middle grades are the most critical time period in the development of student attitudes toward mathematics.

4. Extremely positive or negative attitudes tend to predict mathematics achievement better than more neutral attitudes.

5. Gender-related differences in attitudes towards mathematics exist, perhaps related to similar gender-related differences in confidence or anxiety measures relative to learning mathematics.

Students develop positive attitudes toward mathematics when they perceive mathematics as useful and interesting. Similarly, students develop negative attitudes towards mathematics when they do not do well or view mathematics as uninteresting. Furthermore, high school students' perceptions about the usefulness of mathematics affect their decisions to continue to take elective mathematics courses.

High levels of positive feeling toward mathematics and intrinsic motivation are important prerequisites for student creativity, student use of diverse problem solving strategies, and deep understanding of mathematics. Elementary students think that mathematics is difficult. In fact, if something is easy, they conclude that it cannot involve mathematics. As they get older and the once difficult mathematics now seems easy, students adjust their view of mathematics to ensure that it is difficult and unfamiliar.

Research on student locus-of-control has revealed a growing amount of "fatalism" in middle school mathematics classrooms that seems to persist through high school. Students state that they are "not in control" when they try to solve a mathematics problem, as "something or somebody else pulls all the strings." Furthermore, the attitude can develop into a belief that they cannot solve mathematics problems.

The development of positive mathematical attitudes is linked to the direct involvement of students in activities that involve both quality mathematics and communication with significant others within a clearly defined community such as a classroom.

Students rapidly lose or ignore meaning in mathematics when in middle school, a time when symbols take on "a life of their own" with few connections being made to conceptual representations. The result is an overuse of rote rules or procedures with no effort on the students' part to evaluate the reasonableness of any answers they obtain.

Students believe that mathematics is important, difficult, and based on rules. Similarly, students associate mathematics with uncertainty, with knowing, and being able to get the right answer quickly. In turn, Lampert suggests that "these cultural assumptions are shaped by school experience, in which doing mathematics means remembering and applying the correct rule when the teacher asks a question, and mathematical truth is determined when the answer is ratified by the teacher".

Students' beliefs about mathematics can weaken their ability to solve nonstandard problems in mathematics. For example, if students believe that they should be able to complete every mathematics problem in five minutes or less, they will not persevere when trying to solve a problem that requires more than five minutes. The problem is that these beliefs are built from their perceptions of mathematics that is experienced continually in classroom situations.

Teachers confront "critical moments" in their mathematics classroom by making decisions that reflect their personal beliefs about mathematics and how it should be taught. Student attitudes toward mathematics correlate strongly with their mathematics teacher's clarity (e.g., careful use of vocabulary and discussion of both the why and how during problem solving) and ability to generate a sense of continuity between the mathematics topics in the curriculum.

The attitude of the mathematics teacher is a critical ingredient in the building of an environment that promotes problem solving and makes students feel comfortable to talk about their mathematics. Many students respond intensely and negatively when they confront word problems that involve multiplying or dividing by decimals less than one. This negative reaction is triggered by the students' solution process because it contradicts their expectations that in mathematics "multiplication makes bigger, division makes smaller".

Students who attribute their success in mathematics to high ability or effort will be motivated to learn mathematics. In contrast, students who attribute their lack of success in mathematics to low ability or the material's difficulty will not be motivated to study mathematics and expect not to be able to learn mathematics. Mathematics teachers need to intervene to help the unmotivated students realise that success in learning mathematics is related to effort.

Teaching children to both set personal learning goals and take responsibility for their own learning of mathematics leads to increased motivation and higher achievement in mathematics.Teacher feedback to students is an important factor in a student's learning of mathematics. Students who perceive the teacher's feedback as being "controlling and stressing goals that are external to them" will decrease their intrinsic motivation to learn mathematics. However, students who perceive the teacher's feedback as being "informational" and that it can be used to increase their competence will increase their intrinsic motivation to learn mathematics.

Mathematics teachers need to focus their students' motivation and persistence on both "deriving meaning from the mathematics task rather than just getting the task done" and "developing independent thinking skills and strategies for solving mathematics problems rather than on obtaining the one right answer to the mathematics problem" Peterson.

Teacher feedback to students is an important factor in a student's learning of mathematics. Students who perceive the teacher's feedback as being "controlling and stressing goals that are external to them" will decrease their intrinsic motivation to learn mathematics. However, students who perceive the teacher's feedback as being "informational" and that it can be used to increase their competence will increase their intrinsic motivation to learn mathematics.

Mathematics teachers need to focus their students' motivation and persistence on both"deriving meaning from the mathematics task rather than just getting the task done and developing independent thinking skills and strategies for solving mathematics problems rather than on obtaining the one right answer to the mathematics problem.

8

Cognitive and Social Development of Students

Education is widely recognised as the most important pathway to prepare young people for healthy and productive adult lives. Historically, formal education began at age 6 with entry into first grade, but over the last few decades, most children begin formal school with entry into kindergarten, typically at age 5. With the increase in women who work outside of the home, more and more children now receive child care outside of the home prior to beginning kindergarten, with much of this care taking place in center-based programs.

Preschools differ widely in their purposes and the types of experiences they provide young children. The differences can be characterised by two widely used terms, child care and preschool, with the former suggesting an environment primarily oriented towards caring for children and the latter suggesting an environment more oriented to formal learning.

There has been in the past a sharp distinction between child care, i.e., full-day programs of care for children whose parents are working, and preschool, i.e., halfday programs focused on children's social and academic learning, but this is changing. Child care professionals increasingly define their mission in educational terms, with growing support from parents and educators. This does not mean that child care should be devoted to academic training for children under 5 any more than preschool. The developing consensus is that out-of-home care for young children should attend to their education, including school readiness, as well as providing protection and a facilitating environment for secure emotional development and sound relationships with other children and adults.

One of the reasons for the increased attention on preschools is that a growing body of research evidence finds that good experiences in quality preschool programs can have a positive impact on school readiness in kindergarten and long-term performance in school. Yet access to preschools varies widely among children from different racial, ethnic, and social class backgrounds. These differences in preschool participation may be contributing to the achievement gap by providing better preparation for kindergarten to middle-income students than to low-income minority students.

Although much of the attention on disparities in preschool participation and school achievement has focused on racial and ethnic groups, another important demographic group is the growing population of language minority children. For example in United States, according to figures from the 2000 Census, almost 10 million children ages five to seventeen-18 percent of the population-spoke a language other than English at home. More than two-thirds of these children spoke Spanish. In some states, the proportion of language minority or bilingual children is much greater. California is home to the largest number and largest concentration of language minority children in the U.S.—more than 2.8 million children, or 43 percent of the population spoke a non-English language at home in 2000. In five other states—Arizona, Nevada, New Mexico, New York, and Texas—the concentration of language minority children exceeded 25 percent of the population.

Although some language minority children enter school already proficient in English (FEP—fluent English proficient), most are not yet proficient and are referred to as English language learners (ELLs). Research demonstrates that language minority students, both those who are fluent when they enter school and those who are not, have lower academic achievement than students from English-only backgrounds. For example, a recent study that compared the four-year growth rates in reading scores among three cohorts of California English-only and language minority students, both FEP and ELL, found a sizeable and increasing achievement gap as students progress through school. The achievement gap in other subjects is similar. But language groups vary by other characteristics related to school performance, such as income and parental education, so it is often difficult to determine whether these differences are related to language background and English proficiency or other, related demographic factors.

Preschool may provide a useful strategy for improving school readiness for all students and reducing initial achievement differences among social groups, including language groups. But as in the case of ethnic, racial, and social class groups, preschool may also be contributing to the achievement gap. One of the limitations of existing research on preschools is that language minority students are frequently not included in the studies. For example, two of the largest studies of child care experiences in the U.S., the Cost, Quality, and Outcomes Study and the National Institute for Child Health and Development (NICHD) Study of Early Child Care, only include families who speak English.

Study on Children's Preschool Participation

A recent research study on the cognitive and social development of language minority students, conducted by Russell W. Rumberger and Loan Tran, in support of National Center for Research on Evaluation, Standards, and Student Testing (CRESST)/University of California examined participation in preschool and its relationship with the cognitive and social development of language minority students. The study was able to overcome many of the limitations of previous studies. The data used in the study came from the Early Childhood Longitudinal Study of the Kindergarten Class of 1998-99 (ECLS-K) and included a representative sample of students and parents who did not speak English. Parent interviews were conducted primarily via telephone with bilingual staff, so only one percent of the parent interviews could not be conducted because of language problems. The direct math assessment was conducted in both English and Spanish, which thereby included the majority of non-English speaking language minority students. And teachers were asked to assess students' cognitive skills irrespective of language. The study was able to generate considerable and valuable information on preschool participation and its relationship with school outcomes. The detail of the study —its methodology and finding— are discussed in this chapter to find out the cognitive and social development of pre-school students.

The study was based on data from the Early Childhood Longitudinal Study Kindergarten cohort (ECLS-K). ECLS-

K is a national sample of about 20,000 kindergarteners that entered about 1,000 public and private schools in the fall of 1998 and are being tracked as they progress through school. Two samples of data from ECLS-K were used in the study: a cross-sectional sample of students, parents, teachers and schools from the initial wave of the study in the fall of kindergarten; and a longitudinal subsample of students that were tracked until third grade. The first sample was used to address the first two research questions that focused on preschool participation and its relationship with kindergarten school readiness; the second sample was used to address the third research question that focused on third-grade school performance. Child-level weights, which adjusted for differences in selection and response, were used to generate accurate population estimates.

The language background of the students in both samples was determined from several questions in the fall kindergarten parent questionnaire. First, all parents were asked, "Is any language other than English regularly spoken in your home?". If the answer was affirmative, the student was identified as "language minority"; otherwise the student was identified as "non-language minority". Second, parents who indicated another language was spoken were asked, "What languages other than English were spoken in your home?". Third, parents who indicated another language was spoken were also asked, "What is the primary language spoken in your home?. Students whose parents indicated that English was the primary language spoken at home were classified as "English dominant." Students from Spanish-speaking households whose parents indicated that English was NOT the primary language were identified as "Spanish dominant." Students from non-Spanish-speaking households whose parents indicated that English was NOT the primary language were identified as "Other dominant."

Both samples contain sizeable and representative samples of language minority students. According to these figures, more than 22 percent of kindergarteners in the fall of 1998 came from a home where a language other than English was spoken. More than 10 percent of all students, or almost half of all language minority students, came from homes where English was the primary language. Of the remaining language minority students, the vast majority came from households where Spanish was the primary language.

The ECLS-K data provide measures of students' academic, social, and physical development as they progress through elementary school and extensive data on their background as well as the characteristics of their families, teachers, and schools. These data were collected from:

- *Direct assessments of children's cognitive, psychomotor, and physical skills and characteristics:* These assessments were obtained through untimed, one-on-one, computer-assisted interviews. The cognitive assessment focused on three general areas of competence: (1) language use and literacy; (2) mathematics; and (3) knowledge of the social and physical world, referred to as "general knowledge." These assessments were conducted in the fall of kindergarten, spring of kindergarten, fall of first grade, spring of first grade, and spring of third grade. Children who were identified by the school as language minority were given a brief language screener, the Oral Language Development Scale (OLDS). Children who were determined to be proficient in English, based on the screener, were given the full direct assessment battery. Children from a Spanish background who were not proficient in English where given the mathematics and psychomotor assessments in Spanish. Children from a non-Spanish background who were not proficient in English were excluded from the cognitive assessments.

– *Parent/guardian questionnaires:* Parents were asked to provide key information about their children, especially during the first years of the study. Information was collected from parents each time children were assessed using computer-assisted telephone interviewing (CATI) or computer-assisted personal interviewing (CAPI) if they did not have a telephone.

– *Teacher questionnaires:* Teachers were not only asked to provide information about their own backgrounds, teaching practices, and experience, they were also called upon to provide information on the classroom setting for the sampled children they teach and to evaluate each sampled child on a number of critical cognitive and non-cognitive dimensions. Teachers completed self-administered questionnaires each time children were assessed, with the exception of the fall first grade data collection.

– *School administrator questionnaires:* School administrators were asked to complete self-administered questionnaires during the spring data collection. They were asked to provide information on the physical, organisational, and fiscal characteristics of their schools, and on the schools' learning environment and programs.

The data were used to create a number of dependent and independent variables:

Dependent variables: The study created a number of dependent variables to measure students' cognitive and social development, and school performance in school:

- Direct assessments of cognitive development: reading, mathematics, and science (third grade);
- Teacher assessments of academic performance: language and literacy, mathematics, general knowledge (kindergarten), science (third grade), and social studies (third grade);
- Teacher assessments of five measures of social development, which were developed from the Social Skills Rating System developed by Gresham and Elliot: approaches to learning, self-control, social interaction, internal problem behaviours, and external problem behaviours;
- Direct assessments of students' social-emotional development in six areas: their perceived competence and interest in reading, mathematics, and school in general, their perceived competence and popularity with peers, and their reported problems with their external and internal behaviour;
- School record data indicating whether the student was retained, below grade level, or was identified as a special education student since entering kindergarten.

Independent variables. The study team created a number of independent variables in three broad categories. First, the study team created variables collected from parents in the fall kindergarten questionnaire about their current child care arrangements and arrangements the year prior to entering kindergarten, including:

- Who provided child care (relatives, non-relatives, Head Start, or non-Head Start center);

– Age when child first attended;
– Number of different providers child attended;
– Type of program;
– Number of children and adults in child's room or group;
– Hours per week and length of time child attended;

Second, the study team created two sets of language measures: one set simply identified students as language minorities or non-language minorities. Then the study team created a series of three sub-groups of language minorities: students from English-dominant households, students from Spanishdominant households, and students from other-language-dominant households. Finally, the study uses a number of family and student characteristics in the statistical models to differentiate the effects of language background from the effects of other, related characteristics:

– Family socioeconomic status;
– Family structure (not living with both biological parents);
– Number of children in the home less than 18 years of age;
– Number of books in the household;
– Mother's working status;
– Child has a disability

These particular variables were selected because they primarily represent stable characteristics of students and families that likely existed prior to preschool, and that prior research suggests could be associated both with participation in preschool and performance in school.

Controlling for these characteristics in the statistical models of school readiness and third grade performance provides more accurate estimates of the effects of language background and preschool.

Two types of analyses were conducted to address the research questions in the study. First, the study team computed descriptive statistics to examine differences in preschool participation, school readiness, and third grade school performance by language background. Second, the study team developed and tested a series of statistical models to examine predictors of preschool participation and the effects of preschool on kindergarten school readiness and third grade school performance after controlling for the effects of other background characteristics. These models were used to examine the extent to which these outcomes were directly related to language background versus other, related factors.

Language background is related to a number of other demographic characteristics. Two important ones are race/ethnicity and income/socioeconomic status. Language background varies widely between race and ethnic groups. White and black kindergarteners overwhelmingly come from non-language minority backgrounds, while Asian and Hispanic kindergartners come from predominantly non-English backgrounds. Family income, poverty, and socioeconomic status also vary greatly, but only among some language minority groups. Overall, language minority children come from families with lower income and socioeconomic status than children from English-only backgrounds. But children from Spanish-dominant households have much lower income and socioeconomic status than children from English-dominant or other-language-dominant households.

Early Care and Education

In the fall of 1998 parents in the ECLS-K study were asked a series of questions about their child care arrangements. They were asked whether their kindergartener was currently receiving or had ever received care from: (1) relatives; (2) non-relatives in a private home; or attended: (3) Head Start; (4) day-care center, nursery school, preschool, or prekindergarten program other than Head Start. Parents also were asked whether their child received care at or attended these programs on a regular basis the year before kindergarten.

Parents reported that their kindergarteners had participated in a number of child care arrangements: 43 percent had received care from relatives, 36 percent had received care from non-relatives, and 77 percent had attended some sort of preschool program, including Head Start. These arrangements varied by language background. Fewer language minority children received non-relative care and attended preschool than non-language minority children.

But there were also differences among language minority children: Kindergarteners from English-dominant households were the most likely to attend preschool, kindergarteners from Spanish-dominant households were the least likely to attend preschool, and kindergarteners from other-language-dominant households were between these two groups. There were also differences in the type of preschool attended-language minority children were more likely to attend Head Start programs whereas non-language minority children were more likely to attend non-Head Start programs.

Similar differences appear with respect to child care arrangements the year before kindergarten. Overall, 68 percent of kindergarteners attended preschool the year before kindergarten, a figure similar to national estimates from other data sources. Non-languageminority kindergartners were more likely to attend non-Head Start centers compared to language minority kindergartners, particularly those from Spanish-dominant households, whereas language minority kindergartners were more likely to attend Head Start centers.

Parents whose child attended a non-Head Start program the year before kindergarten were also asked the kind of center program their child attended the most. Overall, half of the parents reported that their child attended a preschool, 28 percent reported that their child attended a pre-kindergarten program, 18 percent reported that their child attended a day care center, and 4 percent reported that their child attended a nursery school. These patterns were similar across language groups.

Table 1. Type of non-Head Start program attended most the year before kindergarten by language background, fall 1998 kindergarteners (Percent distribution)

	Day care center	*Nursery school*	*Preschool program*	*Pre-K*
Total	18	4	50	28
Non-language-minority	19	3	51	27
Language minority	15	3	48	34
English dominant	15	4	48	33
Spanish dominant	13	2	45	39
Other dominant	22	3	52	23

Many parents reported using more than one type of child care arrangement. Based on the number of hours per week that parents reported for each type, it was possible to determine the primary type of non-parental care that children received the year before kindergarten.

The results show that preschool was the dominant form of non-parental care for kindergarteners overall, but again language minorities and Spanish-dominant language minorities were more likely to attend Head Start programs and less likely to attend non-Head Start programs than non-language minority students. In addition, language minority kindergarteners, particularly Spanish-dominant language minorities, were more likely to have only parental care the year before kindergarten.

Exposure to Preschool

It is also useful to examine how much time children spent in preschool the year before kindergarten. The results show that 43 percent of kindergartners who attended Head Start programs were there 20 hours or more per week, and 40 percent of children who attended non-Head Start programs were there 20 hours or more per week. Among those who attended Head Start, non-language-minority students were more likely to attend more than 20 hours (50 percent) compared to language minority students (31 percent), with students from Spanish-dominant households the least likely to attend more than 20 hours (27 percent).

Among those who attended non-Head Start programs, patterns were similar across language groups. Parents of kindergartners who attended non-Head Start programs the year before kindergarten were also asked how many months their child attended. The vast majority of children (81 percent) attended nine to 12 months, or most of the year. These patterns were also similar across language groups.

Table 2. Months attended non-Head Start program the year before kindergarten by language background, fall 1998 kindergarteners (Percent distribution)

	Months			
	1-2	3-5	6-8	9-12
Total	1	4	14	81
Non-language minority	1	4	15	80
Language minority	2	4	13	81
English dominant	1	4	13	82
Spanish dominant	2	5	12	80
Other dominant	3	4	12	81

Parents were also asked how old their kindergartner was when he or she first attended preschool on a regular basis. The majority of kindergartners who attended Head Start programs first attended at age 4, whereas the majority of kindergartners who attended non-Head Start programs started before age 4, with more than one-third starting before age 3. In general, language minority kindergartners were more likely to first enroll in preschool at an older age thaı: non-language minority kindergartners, with the greatest disparities for Spanishdominant language minorities.

Predicting Preschool Participation

The preceding descriptive statistics show that language minority students were more likely to attend Head Start preschool programs and less likely to attend non-Head Start preschool programs the year before kindergarten than non-language-minority students. But what accounts for those differences-were they directly related to the language background of students or other, related demographic characteristics, such as socioeconomic status (SES)? To address this question, the study team developed and estimated a series of statistical models to predict preschool attendance the year before kindergarten. In particular, the models predicted the change in odds of attending a Head Start program or a non-Head Start program versus some other form of care associated with each predictor variable in the model controlling for the effects of the other predictor variables. The change in odds is expressed as a ratio that can vary from less than one to greater than one.

A value of one signifies no significant change in the odds or likelihood of attending a preschool program versus some other form of care, while a value greater than one indicates an increased likelihood, and a value less than one indicates a decreased likelihood. First, the study team estimated a model that predicted the relative odds of language minority students attending Head Start or non-Head Start preschool programs compared to non-language minority students with no other variables in the model. The results show that the odds of a language minority student attending Head Start relative to the odds of a non-language minority student attending Head Start are 1.29 or 29 percent higher. In contrast, the odds of a language minority student attending a center-based program relative to the odds of a non-language minority student attending are .64, or 36 percent less.

These results confirm the descriptive findings presented earlier that show language minority students are more likely to be enrolled in Head Start programs and less likely to be enrolled in non-Head Start programs than non-language minority students. The next model added a series of other predictor variables to the model. The results show that a number of other variables predict whether students attended Head Start or non-Head Start programs the year before kindergarten. Students from high SES families were less likely to attend Head Start and more likely to attend preschools than students from low SES families.

Students with mothers who were currently working full time or part time were less likely to attend either Head Start or non-Head Start programs the year before kindergarten compared to students with mothers who were not working. Students in families with more children and in non-traditional families were more likely to have attended Head Start, and less likely to have attended non-Head Start programs. The study team also analysed the effects of two neighborhood variables—the number of preschools per 1000 children and the mean SES of the community. The availability of preschools had a small positive effect of attendance in Head Start and center programs. Community SES was a sizeable predictor-students who lived in high SES communities were less likely to attend Head Start and more likely to attend non-Head Start programs, even controlling for the availability of all preschools.

This may reflect the influence of neighbors on desirability of non-Head Start programs versus Head Start, or the greater likelihood of centers versus Head Start programs in higher SES communities. After controlling for these family background and community characteristics, the odds of language minority students attending Head Start programs the year before kindergarten were the same as non-language minority students. In contrast, the odds of language minority students attending non-Head Start programs remained almost the same. That is, language minority students were less likely to attend center-based programs than non-languageminority students, even after controlling for a number of family background and community variables.

The study team then estimated a second set of similar models to see whether preschool attendance varied among the three language minority subgroups-English dominant, Spanish dominant, and other language dominant-first with no control variables in the models and then with the same set of control variables as earlier.

The results show that preschool participation varied widely among the three language subgroups. English-dominant students were just as likely as non-language minority students to attend Head Start programs, but less likely to attend non-Head Start programs, even after controlling for other factors.

Spanishdominant students were more likely than non-language minority students to attend Head Start programs, but just as likely after controlling for other factors. Spanish-dominant students were 60 percent less likely than non-language minority students to attend non-Head Start programs and were 40 percent less likely after controlling for other factors,. Other-language-dominant students were 67 percent more likely than non-language minority students to attend Head Start with and without controlling for other factors.

Conversely, other-language-dominant students were about 25 percent less likely than non-language minority students to attend non-Head Start programs, even after controlling for other factors. These results confirm the descriptive findings-language minorities as a group were less likely than non-language minority students to attend non-Head Start preschool programs the year before kindergarten, with Spanish-dominant language minority students even less likely than English-dominant and other-language-dominant students.

Relationship between Preschool and School Readiness

The second issue addressed in the study is the relationship between preschool and school readiness at the beginning of kindergarten. Previous research has suggested that students who attend preschool are more likely than other students to have mastered some preliminary skills in reading and math, and to display proper social behaviors conducive to school learning.

Do students in the ECLS dataset show similar patterns? And do language minority students show similar patterns compared to non-language minority students? To answer these questions, the study team first analysed differences in school readiness by preschool participation and language background. The study team examined both cognitive dimensions of school readiness and social dimensions based on the direct cognitive assessments administered by ECLS field staff and on teacher assessments of classroom academic performance and social behavior. They also examined two other education outcomes: kindergarten retention and identified special education. Next, they tested a series of statistical models to determine the effects of language background and other factors on school readiness.

English Proficiency

One of the major challenges facing language minority students is becoming fluent in English. English fluency allows language minority students to fully comprehend and benefit from the language of instruction, which in most classrooms in America is English. Typically, English-proficient students do not need nor require additional support to learn and succeed in school. In contrast, language minority students who enter school not proficient in

English, who are often referred to as English language learners, often cannot comprehend the language of instruction in English classrooms and, therefore, cannot learn at the same rate as other students without sufficient support in the form of specialised classroom materials, appropriate modes of instruction, and adequate teacher knowledge.

English fluency is typically assessed when students first enter school. In ECLS-K, students were identified as language minority by a number of means, with the most common being a language survey given to parents when they registered their child for kindergarten. The surveys ask a series of questions about the language background of the child and of the child's home, such as the child's first language and whether anyone in the home speaks a language other than English. About half of the parents in ECLS-K completed the home language survey. If no language survey was available, teachers or other school personnel determined language background. Students identified by the school as language minority were given a brief language screener, the Oral Language Development Scale (OLDS), which measured their oral English proficiency.

Only 52 percent of all language minority students took the OLDS, which means that the schools identified a language minority population about half the size that the study team did based on the parent questionnaire. This may be attributable to the fact that only about half of the parents filled out a language survey when they enrolled their child in school. As a result, schools may not have had an accurate way of identifying the language background or English proficiency of their entering students, or some parents-concerned that their child may be identified as language minority and placed in a bilingual classroom-may have intentionally not identified the language background of their child when they enrolled them in school. For whatever reason, the estimates of the language minority population are much larger than estimates based on school records, an issue that is worthy of further study.

Only 21 percent of students from English-dominant households were identified by their schools as a language minority and were administered the language screener, but 83 percent of those students were classified as English proficient. In contrast, 84 percent of the students from Spanish-dominant households were identified by their schools as a language minority, and only 31 percent of those students were classified as English proficient. Finally, 69 percent of students from other-language-dominant households were identified by their schools as a language minority and were administered the language screener, and 65 percent of those students were classified as English proficient. Rates of English proficiency varied among language minority students based on their preschool experience. Whereas students from other-language-dominant households who attended non-Head Start programs had higher rates of English proficiency than students from other-language-dominant households who attended Head Start or did not attend preschool, this relationship did not apply to either English-dominant or Spanish-dominant students.

Cognitive Skills

Cognitive skills were assessed in two ways-through a direct assessment administered one-on-one by ECLS-K field staff, and through a teacher evaluation. For language minority students, the direct assessment of cognitive skills was only conducted if the students were classified as English proficient based on the language screener, with the exception of Spanish-speaking students, who were given the mathematics assessment in Spanish.

In contrast, the teachers were asked to assess the cognitive skills of all students, no matter what their language background. In fact, the teacher questionnaire explicitly stated:

> Children with Limited English Proficiency: Please answer the questions based on your knowledge of this child's skills. If the child does not yet demonstrate skills in English but does demonstrate them in his/her native language, please answer the questions with the child's native language in mind.

Moreover, teachers were asked to evaluate their students on all four modalities of literacy: oral comprehension, oral expression, reading, and writing. As a result, the teacher assessments provide a more comprehensive measure of language minority students' cognitive skills, especially in literacy. The study team analysed differences in cognitive skills by language background and preschool participation, focusing on reading and mathematics, the two core subjects taught in early elementary school.

For each subject area, an overall score was calculated for each student. The study team normalised these scores so that the mean score for the entire population of kindergarteners was 0 and the standard deviation was 1. This allows easy comparisons among different groups and different assessments using a common metric-standard deviations, sometimes referred to as effect sizes. Additionally, the results of the assessments were used to determine whether the students were proficient in performing a series of specific skills related to that area.

First, the study team examine the results from the direct assessments and then the results from the teacher assessments.

The direct assessment in reading shows widespread differences by language background and preschool participation. Overall, mean reading scores for language minority students are.17 standard deviations (SD) below the mean for all kindergarteners, or .19 SD below the mean for non-language minority students. Although there are no strict standards to interpret these values, values above .8 SD are often considered large, values above .5 are considered moderate, values above .2 SD are considered small, and values below .2 are considered inconsequential. Based on these criteria, this difference is inconsequential.

Differences among language minority groups are much larger, however. While reading scores for English-dominant students are similar to those for non-language-minority students, scores for Spanish-dominant students are more than .5 SD below those of non-language minority students, a moderately large gap. In contrast, mean reading scores for other-language-dominant groups are somewhat larger than those of non-language minority students. Of course these comparisons only include language-minority students who took and passed the language screener, so they represent only a subset of all language minority students. Reading scores also varied widely by preschool experience. Students who attended Head Start programs the year before kindergarten had mean reading scores one-quarter of a standard deviation (-.51 - [-.26] = -.25) lower than students without preschool experience. In contrast, students who attended non-Head Start programs the year before kindergarten had reading scores one-third of a standard deviation higher (.17 - [-.26] =.43).

For the most part, these patterns were similar across language groups; that is, students from each language group who attended Head Start programs had lower reading scores than students who did not attend preschool, while students who attended non-Head Start programs had higher reading scores. There was only one exception: Spanish-dominant language minority students who attended Head Start programs had similar reading scores as Spanish-dominant students who did not attend preschool.

Additionally, the difference in reading scores between students who attended non-Head Start programs and students who did not attend preschool was generally larger for language minority students than for non-language-minority students. For example, the difference was.39 SD (=.17 - [-.22]) for non-language minority students, compared to.52 SD (=.19 - [-.33]) for English-dominant students, .30 SD (= -.35 - [-.65]) for Spanish-dominant students, and .82 SD (=.62 - [-.20]) for other-language-dominant students. This suggests that non-Head Start programs have a higher relative benefit for language minority students than for non-language minority students.

These patterns are also apparent in specific reading skills. Of course, all these comparisons do not consider other factors that may be related to both preschool attendance and language background, such as socioeconomic status. Later in this chapter, the study team present statistical models that isolate the effects of language background from other, related factors.

Differences in direct-assessed math scores by language background and preschool experience show similar patterns as those discussed above. The only exception is that math scores, compared to reading, for Spanish-dominant students are even lower than scores for other language groups,, and the relative benefit of attending non-Head Start programs is less than for any other language group. For example, the difference in math scores between Spanishdominant students who attended non-Head Start programs the year before kindergarten and those who did not attend preschool was.24 SD (= -.58 - [-.82]), whereas the difference was.47 SD (=.14 - [-.33]) for English-dominant students and.55 SD (=.51 -.04) for other-languagedominant students.

The difference in the scores between reading and math for Spanish-dominant students can probably be attributed to the fact that almost all Spanish-dominant students were assessed in math because a Spanish-language version of the assessment was provided, whereas only those Spanish-dominant students who were proficient in English were given the reading assessment. In contrast, students from other-dominant-language backgrounds were only given the math assessment if they were proficient in English.

The teacher assessments of cognitive performance, as mentioned above, were conducted for all students no matter what their level of English proficiency, so they probably provide a more comprehensive picture of the cognitive performance of language minority students. Differences in mean literacy scores and skill proficiencies by language background and preschool experience look more similar to the directly-assessed math results, which included more language minority students, than to the directly-assessed reading results, which excluded more language minority students. Overall, mean literacy scores for language minority students were.43 SD lower than mean literacy scores for non-language minority students (= -.33 - [-.10]), a gap more similar to the one from the direct math assessment (.39 SD), than the direct reading assessment (.19 SD). Differences in literacy scores by preschool experience and among language groups are very similar to the differences based on the direct cognitive assessments.

Scores on teacher-assessed math skills show similar patterns, although the achievement gaps are generally lower in math than in literacy. For example, the difference between language minority students and non-language-minority students in mean math scores was.34 SD (= -.26 - [-.08]), compared to a gap of. 43 SD in literacy.

Social Skills

In addition to cognitive skills, kindergarten teachers assessed the social skills of their students in five areas. In general, differences in social skills by language background and preschool experience are similar to those the study team observe with respect to cognitive skills, but the differences are much smaller and therefore not meaningful in most cases. For example, the overall difference in social skills between non-language minority and language minority students was less than.1 SD and therefore should be considered inconsequential. Differences in social skills between students who attended Head Start the year before kindergarten and students who did not attend any preschool were small (about.3 SD), while the differences between students who attended non-Head Start programs and students who did not attend preschool were inconsequential (less than.1 SD).

Special Education

The study team also examined differences in kindergarten retention and referrals to special education by language background and preschool participation. The results do not show widespread differences in kindergarten retention rates by language background or preschool participation. There were more pronounced differences in the percent of students identified as special education after enrolling in school, by preschool participation.

Whereas only two percent of students who attended non-Head Start preschool programs were identified as special education, five percent of students who attended Head Start programs were identified as special education. Similar differences were observed for nonlanguage-minority and English-dominant students, but there were no differences among students from Spanish-dominant and other-language-dominant households.

School Readiness

The descriptive statistics presented earlier showed large differences in cognitive skills between kindergarten students who attended preschool and students who did not attend preschool. Students who attended non-Head Start programs showed higher levels of cognitive skills, while students who attended Head Start programs showed lower levels of cognitive skills compared to students who did not attend any form of preschool. However, these differences may not be due to the effects of preschool itself; rather, they could be due to differences in characteristics of students and their families who were able to afford-and who chose to attend-preschool.

For example, if more advantaged families-those with higher incomes and more educated parents-were more likely to enroll their children in non-Head Start programs and where also more likely to improve the cognitive skills of their children through family resources and activities, then some of the observed differences between students with and without non-Head Start preschool could be related to family background differences and not preschool itself.

Similarly, if more disadvantaged parents were more likely to enroll their children in Head Start programs and were also less likely to improve the cognitive skills of their children because of a lack of family resources, then some of the observed differences between students with and without Head Start could be related to family background differences. These differences are known as selection effects. In order to estimate the effect of preschool on school readiness, it is important to control for selection effects, or the effects of family background that could influence both participation in preschool and school readiness.

The simplest way to do this is to use a statistical model that predicts the effects of preschool controlling for family background variables. This is the method the study team used. In conducting this analysis the study team focused on initial literacy scores assessed by students' kindergarten teachers because this school readiness measure had the most valid responses for language minority students. Recall that language minorities who were not proficient in English were excluded from the direct assessments, whereas teachers assessed all students in their literacy and math skills.

The study team first estimated a model examining the effects of Head Start programs and non-Head Start programs on literacy scores without controlling for any other variables in the model. The results, show that students who attended non-Head Start preschool programs had literacy scores that were.41 standard deviations (SD) higher than students who did not attend any preschool. These results are similar to what the study team observed with the descriptive data presented earlier. However, students who attended Head Start programs had literacy scores that were.21 SD lower than students who did not attend preschool. Next, the study team introduced a series of control variables that the study team found in earlier analyses were predictive of preschool participation.

Recall, for example, that increases in family SES increased the likelihood of attending non-Head Start programs and decreased the likelihood of attending Head Start; increases in family SES are associated with higher literacy scores, even after controlling for the effects of preschool. Similarly, language minority students were less likely to attend non-Head Start preschool programs and also had lower literacy scores at the beginning of kindergarten even after controlling for the effects of other predictor variables such as SES.

Whereas literacy scores for language minority students from English-dominant households were only slightly lower (-.14 SD), literacy scores for language minority students from Spanish-dominant households were moderately lower (-.45 SD) and literacy scores for language minority students from otherlanguage-dominant households were somewhat lower (-.24 SD). Several other variables that were associated with preschool participation were also associated with school readiness. After controlling for all of these variables, the estimated effect of attending a non-Head Start program was reduced from.41 SD to.25 SD.

After controlling for all of these variables, the estimated effect of attending a Head Start program was reduced from -.21 SD to zero. The study team also examined whether the effects of preschool varied for students from different language backgrounds. They found that there were no differential effects of non-Head Start or Head Start programs among language groups. This means that attending non-Head Start preschool programs has similar effects on the school readiness of students from all language backgrounds.

Next the study team examined whether the intensity of preschool participation was associated with school readiness. They created two measures of preschool intensity. The first focused on the amount of preschool students had the year before kindergarten based on the number of hours per week and months over the year that students attended. Students were classified as full-time if they attended more than 20 hours per week and 9 months over the year; otherwise they were classified as part-time. The second focused on the year when they first attended preschool. For students who attended non-Head Start programs, the study team identified students who first attended earlier than age 3, at age 3, or at age 4 or 5. About one-third of the students first attended preschool earlier than age 3, one third first started at age 3, and about one-third first started at age 4 or later. For students who attended Head Start, few started before age 3, so the study team identified students who started Head Start at age 3 or earlier, or at age 4 or later. They found that students who attended non-Head Start programs at an earlier age, or who attended full-time, had higher literacy skills than students who attended at a later age or only part-time.

More specifically, students who first attended non-Head Start programs at age 4 or 5 and attended part-time the year before kindergarten, had literacy skills that were.16 SD higher than students who did not attend preschool. In contrast, students who first attended preschool at age 2 or earlier and attended non-Head Start programs for more than part-time had literacy skills that were.28 SD higher than students who did not attend preschool. In other words, the more time students spent in non-Head Start programs, the higher level of cognitive skills.

Intensity of participation had no association with literacy skills for students who attended Head Start programs the year before kindergarten. The study team also examined a quality dimension of Head Start programs based on the number of adults and the number of children in the Head Start program, since research suggest that smaller classrooms and more adults per student create a higher quality learning environment. But again the study team found nó differences between students who attended high quality Head Start programs and those who attended other Head Start programs.

Finally, ECLS tried to verify whether parents who reported that their child attended Head Start programs actually attended Head Start programs the year before kindergarten. About half of the identified Head Start programs were located and the child's attendance verified; the remaining programs could not be located or the child's attendance could not be verified or it was determined that the program was not actually a Head Start program. The study team found that the predicted effect of Head Start did not differ between students whose attendance could be verified and those whose attendance could not be verified-in both cases there was no significant relationship between Head Start and literacy skills.

The study team also estimated models on three other outcomes: externalising problem behaviors, retention, and identified as special education since starting kindergarten. The study team estimated a similar model as the study team did for literacy, controlling for a set of background variables that also predicted preschool participation. After controlling these variables, the study team found that preschool participation still had a significant effect on each of these outcomes.

The results for externalising problem behaviors show that students who attended both Head Start and non-Head Start preschool programs were more likely to be identified by their kindergarten teachers as having externalising problem behaviors. The effects were small and fairly common across language groups, but not consistently so. Students who attended Head Start programs in the year before kindergarten were 71 percent more likely to exhibit problem behaviors than students who did not attend any preschool, with the exception of students from Spanish-dominant households who were 12 percent less likely to exhibit problem behaviors.

Students who attended non-Head Start programs were 86 percent more likely to exhibit problem behaviors than students who did not attend any preschool, with the exception of students from English-dominant households, who were 15 percent less likely to exhibit problem behaviors.

The effects varied by intensity of participation, but only among students who attended non-Head Start programs. In general, the more time students spent in non-Head Start programs, the more likely they were to exhibit problem behaviors. However, students who first attended non-Head Start programs at age 4 and attended half time or less, were no more likely to exhibit problem behaviors than students who did not attend preschool at all. In contrast, students who attended more than part-time and first attended at age 2 or earlier, were more than twice as likely to exhibit problem behaviors as students who did not attend preschool.

The results for kindergarten retention show that students who attended either Head Start or non-Head Start programs were less likely to be attending kindergarten for the second time, although the size of the effects were quite small. For example, after controlling for other predictor variables, students who attended non-Head Start programs were 34 percent less likely to be repeating kindergarten than students who did not attend any preschool. These effects were the same across language groups. In addition, children from Spanish-dominant households were 34 percent more likely to be repeating kindergarten than non-language minority students.

The results for special education show that students who attended non-Head Start preschools the year before kindergarten were 24 percent less likely than students who did not attend any preschool to be identified as special education during the kindergarten year. There was no effect for Head Start. In addition, students from Spanish-dominant households were 36 percent less likely to be identified as special education during kindergarten, and students from other-language-dominant households were 61 percent less likely than nonlanguage-minority students.

Cognitive Outcomes

The study team examined cognitive outcomes based both on the direct assessments and on assessments conducted by students' third grade teachers. However, due to student mobility and the design considerations of the ECLS-K study that limited access to some students' third grade teachers, there were more valid responses from the direct assessments than from the teacher assessments. Furthermore, virtually all language minority students were proficient in English by third grade.

Reading achievement in the spring of third grade varied by language background and preschool participation. Mean reading scores were about one-third of a standard deviation lower for language minority students than non-language-minority students. But this overall difference masks larger differences among language minority subgroups: students from Spanishdominant households were two-thirds of a standard deviation behind non-language minority students, whereas English-dominant students were only slightly behind, and other-languagedominant students were essentially reading at the same levels.

The reading scores of students who attended non-Head Start programs were.36 SD higher than students who did not attend preschool (.20 - [-.16]), while the reading scores of students who attended Head Start programs were.34 SD lower than students who did not attend preschool (-.50 - [-.16]). There were similar differences across language groups. That is, language minority students who attended non-Head Start programs had higher reading scores than language minority students who did not attend preschool, whereas language minority students who attended Head Start programs had lower reading scores than language minority students who did not attend preschool. The only exception was that Spanish-dominant language minority students who attended Head Start programs had somewhat higher reading scores than Spanish-dominant language minority students who did not attend preschool (.18 = -.56 - [-.74]).

Science and math scores show remarkably similar patterns, although the achievement gap between students from Spanish-dominant households and non-language-minority households is much larger in science than in math.

Teachers' assessments of their students' skills also show similar patterns, but the magnitude of the differences was smaller. For example, whereas Spanish-dominant students were.70 SD behind (= -.63 - [.07]) non-language -minority students in mean directassessed reading scores—a relatively large difference per the convention—they were only.25 SD (=.01 - [-.24]) behind in teacher-assessed reading scores, a small difference. Similarly, whereas the difference in mean direct-assessed reading scores of students who attended non-Head Start programs were.36 SD higher (=.20 - [-.16]) than students who did not attend preschool, the difference in mean teacher-assessed reading scores was only.24 SD higher (=.14 - [-.10]).

Social Outcomes

Two types of social outcomes were assessed in third grade. First, teachers were asked to assess the students in the same five areas of social behavior as they did in kindergarten. Second, field assessors asked students a series of questions regarding their attitudes toward school and classmates, and their social behavior.

Teacher-assessed social skills varied somewhat by language background and preschool participation. Learning behaviors were similar among language groups except that other-language-dominant students had learning behaviors that were.39 SD higher (=.37 - [-.02]) than non-language-minority students. Differences in other social behaviors were much smaller and should be considered inconsequential. Differences in social behaviors between students who attended non-Head Start programs and students who didn't attend any preschool, on average, were inconsequential. However, students who attended Head Start program generally had poorer social behaviors than non-preschool students, although the differences were small (less than.5 SD).

Student reports of their attitudes toward school and their peers, as well as their social behavior, varied little by language background and preschool participation with a few exceptions. One was that language minority students from other-language-dominant households reported lower levels of favorable peer relations than non-language-minority students (.16 SD). Two other exceptions concern differences in students' reports of problematic external (anger/distractibility) and internal (sad/lonely/anxious) behaviors. Spanish-dominant language minority students were twice as likely as non-language minority students (30 percent vs. 15 percent) to report often feeling sad, lonely, or anxious; and third grade students who attended Head Start reported higher levels of problematic external and internal behaviors compared to students who did not attend preschool (19 percent vs. 9 percent), with the biggest differences among non-language-minority students.

Retention and Special Education

The study team also examined differences in retention and referrals to special education by language background and preschool participation. There were negligible differences in the percent of students below grade level by language background, but there were somewhat larger differences by preschool participation. Students who attended non-Head Start programs were less likely to be enrolled below grade level, while students who attended Head Start were more likely to be below grade level, compared to students who did not attend preschool the year before kindergarten, with the largest differences among non-language-minority students. For example, 8 percent of non-language -minority students who attended non-Head Start programs were enrolled below grade level, compared to 16 percent who attended Head Start programs, and 13 percent who did not attend preschool. Differences among language minority students were less pronounced. Language minority students from other-language-dominant households were the least likely to be enrolled below grade level, with the lowest rates among those who did not attend preschool.

Nine percent of all students had been identified as special education since kindergarten, and these rates did not vary widely among language groups and preschool participation. As in the case of retention, the biggest differences were among non-language-minority students, with those who attended Head Start programs having higher rates of identification.

Predicting the Effects of Preschool on Third Grade Outcomes

Observed differences in third grade outcomes among students by language background and preschool participation does not mean those differences were "caused" by language background or preschool participation, rather they could be due to other factors that are associated with them, such as family socioeconomic status. To disentangle these effects, the study team estimated a series of statistical models to predict school outcomes that controlled for some of these other factors to better determine the effects of language background and preschool on school outcomes in third grade.

For cognitive outcomes, the study team used the direct assessments in reading, math, and science, rather than the teacher assessments because teacher assessments were not available for a number of ECLS students who changed residences and schools from the fall of kindergarten to the spring of third grade.

The first model estimated third grade reading performance. The study team first estimated a model examining the effects of non-Head Start programs and Head Start programs on reading scores without controlling for any other variables in the model. The results show that third-grade students who attended non-Head Start programs had literacy scores that were.30 standard deviations (SD) higher, and students who attended Head Start programs had literacy scores that were.37 SD lower, than students who did not attend any preschool. These results are similar to what the study team observed with the descriptive data presented earlier. They are also similar to the predicted effects of preschool on kindergarten literacy scores. That is, it appears that the benefits of non-Head Start preschool are sustained from the beginning of kindergarten to the end of third grade.

Some of the achievement differences among language groups also change between kindergarten and third grade. Whereas English-dominant and other-language-dominant students had lower achievement in kindergarten literacy than non-language-minority students, there were no significant differences in reading achievement by third grade. However, Spanish-dominant students continued to lag, although the gap was reduced slightly from.45 SD in kindergarten literacy to.31 SD in third grade reading. Other background variables that had significant effects on kindergarten literacy had similar or sometimes larger effects on third grade reading. For example, SES had an effect size of.24 SD on kindergarten literacy, but an effect size of.35 SD on third grade reading. Similarly, students who did not live with both biological parents had kindergarten literacy scores that were.13 SD lower than students who lived with both of their biological parents; by third grade, the difference in reading scores was.21 SD. These results suggest that family background continues to influence the achievement of students beyond its effect on school readiness.

The study team estimated identical models for math and science achievement. The results are similar to those for reading-after controlling for background variables, the predicted effects of non-Head Start care become inconsequential. The effects of Head Start, however, remain small and negative. Differences among language groups displayed different patterns than they did in reading. Language minority students from Englishdominant households had similar math and science scores as non-language-minority students. Spanish-dominant students had lower scores than non-language-minority students, but the gap was much smaller in math (-.12 SD) than in science (-.48 SD). Students from other-languagedominant households had similar science scores compared to students from non-language minority households, but they had significantly higher math scores (.25 SD).

For the most part, the effects of Head Start and non-Head start programs did not vary among language groups. The only exception was that Spanish dominant students who attended Head Start programs had significantly higher achievement than Spanish dominant students who did not attend any preschool. For example, while Spanish-dominant students who did not attend preschool had reading scores that were.31 SD below English-only students who did not attend preschool, Spanish-dominant students who attended Head Start programs had reading scores comparable to English-only students who did not attend preschool. Similar effects were observed in math and science. But no differential effects were found for language-minority students who attended non-Head Start programs.

Although the average effect of preschool on cognitive development was inconsequential, it is possible that the effects vary by school. To investigate this issue, the study team modified the statistical model to allow for the two preschool variables-Head Start and non-Head Start programs-to vary between schools. Doing so revealed that there was substantial variation between schools in the estimated effects, especially for Head Start. In some schools, students who attended Head Start programs were doing better (+.33 SD) in reading than students who didn't attend any preschool, while in other schools they were doing substantially worse (-.56 SD). In math and science there was less variation, with virtually no Head Start attendees doing better, but some doing substantially worse. There were similar variations among students who attended non-Head Start programs, although the variation was less.

The study team then estimated statistical models for three other third grade student outcomes: student-reported social behavior (those students who rated their externalising problem(s) as 3 or more, which corresponds to an average rating of "often"), enrolled below grade level, and students identified as special education since starting kindergarten. After controlling for background characteristics, participation in preschool had small or insignificant effects on these outcomes.

The study team found statistically significant, but inconsequential, effects of Head Start on problematic behaviors and no statistically significant effects of non-Head Start preschool programs. They also found that the effects did not vary by language group, but they did vary by intensity and duration. Students who attended non-Head Start programs part-time were less likely to report having problematic behaviors than students who did not attend preschool, while students who attended more than part-time were somewhat more likely to report problematic behavior. For example, students who first attended non-Head Start preschool programs at age 4, less than full time, were 27 percent less likely to report problematic behaviors, while students who attended more than part-time were 15 percent more likely to report problematic behaviors.

Students who attended non-Head Start programs were also 28 percent less likely to be below grade level than students who did not attend preschool; this too is considered a small effect. There were no significant differences for students who attended Head Start programs. One question that is important to investigate is whether the effects of non-Head Start programs are due to cognitive or non-cognitive impacts on school readiness; that is, does participation in non-Head Start preschool programs reduce the likelihood of retention because it improves cognitive performance in kindergarten or because it improves attitudes and behaviors that reduce the likelihood of retention? To examine this issue further, the study team added an additional predictor variable in the statistical model-fall kindergarten literacy. When the study team did so, the estimated effects of non-Head Start preschool were greatly reduced and became insignificant.

This suggests that attending non-Head Start preschool programs reduces retention because of its positive effects on initial literacy levels in kindergarten. Further investigation revealed that the effects of non-Head Start center care varied by language groups. Participation in non-Head Start centers reduced the odds of being below grade level by one-third for all language groups except English-dominant students.

Finally, the study team examined whether the effects varied by intensity and duration of preschool participation. They found that the odds of being below grade level were half as much for students who first attended non-Head Start centers at age 2 or earlier, compared to students who started at age 3 or later. Similar to the earlier analysis, the study team added a predictor variable, fall kindergarten literacy, to this final model to see whether the effects of non-Head Start center care were attenuated. Unlike the previous model, in this case the effects of non-Head Start preschool were reduced by about one-third, but remained significant. This suggests that the effects of non-Head Start preschool were not due to its effects on kindergarten literacy, but may rather be due to effects on other non-cognitive factors. In the last analysis, the study team found that students who attended non-Head Start programs were 22 percent less likely to be identified as a special education student. This effect also appears to be mediated by fall kindergarten literacy. They also found the impact varied among language groups. Students from all language groups were less likely to be in special education if they attended non-Head Start preschool programs, with the exception of Spanish-dominant students who were 68 percent more likely to be in special education compared to Spanish dominant students who did not attend preschool.

Finally, the study team examined whether the effects varied by intensity and duration of preschool participation. They found that the odds of being in special education were lower for students who first attended non-Head Start centers at age 2 or earlier than for students who started at age 3 or later.

Result and Discussion

The study examined participation in preschool and its relationship between the cognitive and social development of language minority students. Although there is a large body of research that demonstrates the cognitive and social benefits of attending preschool , very little of this research has included language minority students, or at least those who do not speak English. The present study, based on ECLS-K data, included a representative sample of students and parents who did not speak English. The study examined three issues: participation in preschool, the relationship between preschool participation and school readiness at entry to kindergarten, and the relationship between preschool participation and school performance in third grade.

Here, the term preschool refers to an array of center-based child care programs including day care centers, nursery schools, pre-kindergarten programs, preschools, and Head Start programs. In most of the analyses, the study team compared students who attended Head Start preschool programs and other (non-Head Start), center-based preschool programs with students who did not attend any preschool programs the year before kindergarten. To better understand the role of language background, the study team identified three sub-groups of language minorities: students from households where English was the primary language spoken (English dominant), students from Spanish-speaking households where English was NOT the primary language (Spanish dominant), and students from non-Spanish-speaking households where English was NOT the primary language (Other language dominant).

Participation

Consistent with previous studies, the stwe found that the majority of students who entered kindergarten in the fall of 1998 had attended some form of preschool the year before entering kindergarten, but participation among language minority children was lower than among non-language minority children, with children from Spanish-dominant households having even lower participation rates. Moreover, language minority children were more likely to attend Head Start programs rather than non-Head Start center-based programs. After controlling for other factors that predicted preschool participation, such as socioeconomic status (SES) and mother's employment, language minority students were still 30 percent less likely to attend non-Head Start programs than non-language-minority students; however, they were just as likely to attend Head Start programs as non-language-minority students. Finally, language minority students, especially those from Spanish-dominant households, were less likely than non-language-minority students to attend non-Head Start programs for more than one year.

School Readiness

The study team found widespread differences in several cognitive and non-cognitive measures of school readiness by language background and preschool participation. At least some of these differences can be attributed to differences in the characteristics of students and their families that may be related both to participation in preschool and to cognitive development in kindergarten. After controlling for the effects of a number of these characteristics in the statistical models, the study team found that students who attended preschool, especially non-Head Start programs, had higher levels of school readiness. But preschool participation was also associated with an increased likelihood of exhibiting external behavior problems. These positive and negative associations apply to all students no matter what their language background with only a few exceptions. They also vary by duration and intensity of participation, with earlier and more intensive participation yielding higher cognitive benefits, but also higher likelihood of problematic behaviors.

Third grade outcomes

Differences in cognitive and social development by language background and preschool participation were still observed four years after starting kindergarten, when most students were finishing third grade. Differences in cognitive development by preschool participation remained modest and were similar to those observed in the fall of kindergarten, but when the study team estimated a statistical model that controlled for the same set of predictors as they did for fall kindergarten scores, the estimated effects of preschool became inconsequential, although still statistically significant. Overall, the cognitive effects of non-Head Start preschool programs were reduced by about half, to inconsequential levels.

The study team did find that the effects of preschool programs, particularly Head Start programs, varied among schools, with preschool-attendees doing better than non-preschool attendees in some schools and worse in others. This finding is consistent with other studies that found Head Start participants in particular are more likely to attend lower quality schools, which may help explain why the cognitive benefits fade over time. It is also consistent with one of the findings of the original Coleman study that public schools have a greater effect on disadvantaged than advantaged students.

The modest effects of preschool compare to large disparities in achievement by language background. Entering school, the achievement levels of language minorities were about.4 SD below non-language minority students. The disparities were somewhat smaller by the end of third grade, about.3 SD. But there were also large differences among language groups, in particular, students from Spanish-dominant households entered kindergarten almost.8 SD behind non-language-minority students in literacy skills, and were still.7 SD behind at the end of third grade. Effects on retention and special education remained small (although larger than the effects on achievement); nonetheless, they did not change appreciably from kindergarten, which suggests they are more likely to be sustained in higher grades.

Comparisons with other studies

The findings from the study are consistent with other studies of preschool. The results are also consistent with two recent studies based on ECLS-K, which found smaller effect sizes of non-Head Start programs in fall kindergarten based on direct-assessed reading and math scores (which excluded non-Englishproficient language minority students) after controlling for a similar, but somewhat larger set of student and family demographic variables. The findings-that the cognitive effects of preschool diminished by the end of third grade-are also consistent with an earlier study using ECLS-K that found the estimated effects of attending non-Head Start preschool were reduced by 60 percent between the fall of kindergarten and the spring of first grade.The study team did find that the noncognitive effects-particularly retention and participation in special education-were greater than the cognitive effects and more likely to be sustained, which is also consistent with the literature. The lack of sustainability is also consistent with reviews of a range of experimental preschool interventions that found the cognitive effects of most interventions had become insignificant two to four years after the intervention ended. The exceptions are long-term, high quality interventions, such as the Carolina Abecedarian Project where students received full-day care for five years prior to entering kindergarten.

Although the study was able to overcome many of the limitations of previous studies by using a dataset that included a representative sample of students and parents who did not speak English and non-English based assessments, the ECLS data still had limitations for conducting a study of preschools. The ECLS data relies on retrospective parent interviews for information on their child's preschool experiences, as such, it is subject to recall error. It also meant there was little information on the quality of the preschools that the child attended, which previous studies have shown impacts student outcomes.

Finally, it meant that it was difficult to control for all of the characteristics of families that could have influenced their decision to send their child to preschool, making it hard to assess the causal impacts of preschool on cognitive and social development. Another national longitudinal study, the Early Childhood Longitudinal Study, Birth Cohort (ECLS-B), is tracking a representative sample of children born in the year 2001. The study will be able to overcome many of the limitations of the ECLS-K dataset by collecting information on preschool participation as it takes place and family characteristics prior to participation. This will allow more accurate estimates of the impact of preschool on children's early childhood development.

The findings from the study suggest that attending preschool can improve the school readiness of language minority students. Currently, however, language minority students are less likely to enroll in preschool, particularly non-Head Start programs that appear to make the biggest educational impact. As a result, preschool attendance fails to reduce the large achievement gap between language minority and non-language minority students that exists at kindergarten entry. Improving access to preschool programs and improving the quality of the programs could help address existing disparities in school readiness. Yet because the achievement impact of preschool appears to diminish during the first four years of school, while the achievement gap-especially for Spanish-dominant language minority students-increases, preschool alone may have limited use as a long-term strategy for improving the achievement gap without strengthening the schools these students attend or without providing additional support during the school years. In other words, preschool should be viewed as part of a more comprehensive and sustained effort to improve the educational outcomes of language minority students.

Bibliography

Albanese, M.A. & Mitchell, S. "Problem-based learning: A review of literature on its outcomes and implementation issues". Academic Medicine, 1993.

Ammon, P. and Hutchinson, B.P. "Promoting the development of teachers' pedagogical conceptions". *The Genetic Epistemologist*, 1989.

Ball, D.L. and Lampert, M. "Multiples of evidence, time and perspective: Revising the study of teaching and learning". *Paper prepared for the Commission on Improving Educational Research*, National Academy of Education. 1998.

Barrows, H. "Problem-based learning in medicine and beyond: A brief overview". In L. Wilkerson & W.H. Gijselaers, (Eds.). Bringing problem-based learning to higher education: Theory and practice. *New Directions for Teaching and Learning*, Number 68. San Francisco: Jossey-Bass. 1996.

Bransford, J.D., Brown, A.L. , and Cocking, R.R. "How people learn: Brain, mind, experience and school". Washington, DC: National Academy Press. 1999.

Cerbin, W. "Advancing the scholarship of teaching: Pursuing the scholarship of teaching in educational psychology". *Paper presented at the 1999 Annual Meeting of the American Educational Research Association*, Montreal, Quebec. 1999.

Cobb, P. & Bowers, J. "Cognitive and situated learning: Perspectives in theory and practice". *Educational Researcher*, 1999.

Gijsaelers, W.H. "Connecting problem-based practices with educational theory". In L. Wilkerson & W.H. Gijselaers, (Eds.). Bringing problem-based learning to higher education: Theory and practice. *New Directions for Teaching and Learning*, Number 68. San Francisco: Jossey-Bass. 1996.

Korthhagen, F.A. & Kessels, J.P. "Linking theory and practice: Changing the pedagogy of teacher education". *Educational Researcher*, 1999.

Kuhn, D. "A developmental model of critical thinking". *Educational Researcher*, 1999.

Marshall, H. "Teaching educational psychology: Learner-centered constructivist perspectives". In N.M. Lambert & B.L. McCombs (Eds.) *How students learn: Reforming schools through learner-centered education*. Washington, DC: American Psychological Association. 1998.

Mayer, R. "Cognitive theory for education: What teachers need to know". In N.M. Lambert & B.L. McCombs (Eds.) How students learn: Reforming schools through learner-centered education. Washington, DC: American Psychological Association. 1998.

Norman,G.R. & Schmidt, H.G. "The psychological basis of problem-based learning: A review of the evidence". *Academic Medicine*, 1992.

Perkins, D.N. & Salomon, G. "Teaching for transfer". *Educational Leadership*. 1988.

Royer, J. "Theories of the Transfer of Learning". *Educational Psychologist*. 1979.

Williams, S.M. & Hmelo, C.E. "Learning through problem solving". *Journal of the Learning Sciences*. 1998.

Wiske, M.S. "Teaching for understanding: Linking research to practice". San Francisco: Jossey-Bass. 1998.

Index